Get ready for... Starters

2nd Edition

OXFORD

UNIVERSITY PRESS

Hello!

Words

1 **Listen and read.** 🔊 1

2 **Write. Then ask and answer.**

My name's _____.

I'm _____.

What's your name?
How old are you?

3 **Can you count to twenty? Listen, point and say.** 🔊 2

4 **Find and say the numbers with your friend.**

One.

Two.

Words

1 **Draw lines from the pictures to the words.**

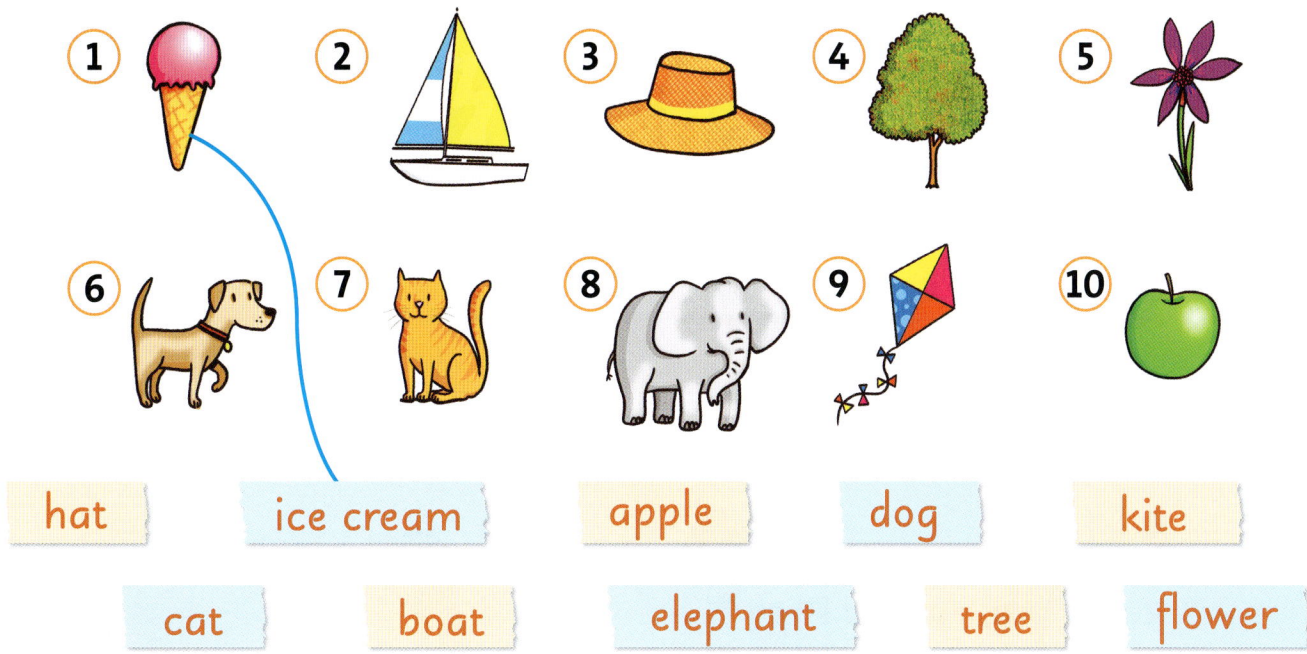

hat   ice cream   apple   dog   kite

cat   boat   elephant   tree   flower

2 **How many are there? Count and write.**

a one	**b**	**c**	**d**
ice cream	elephants	hats	flowers

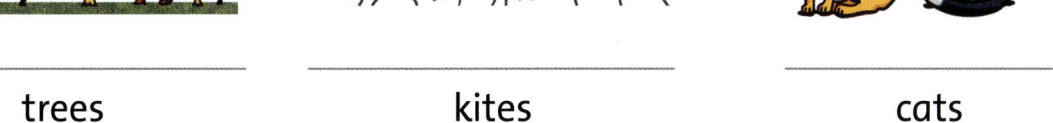

e	**f**	**g**
trees	kites	cats

h	**i**	**j**
apples	dogs	boats

Letters

1 **Look at the letters. Listen and say.** 🔊 **3**

Listen and say the letters with me.

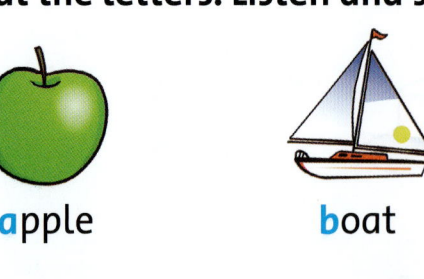

apple

boat

 **c**at

donkey

elephant

fish

 **g**iraffe

house

ice cream

juice

 **k**ite

lorry

mouse

night

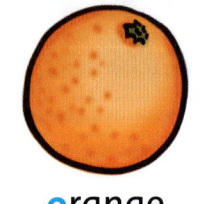 **o**range

plane

question mark

robot

 **s**un

tree

umbrella

vegetables

 **w**atermelon

bo**x**

yellow

zoo

2 **Now say _The Alphabet Rhyme_.** 🔊 **4**

Words

1 Look at the colours and draw lines.

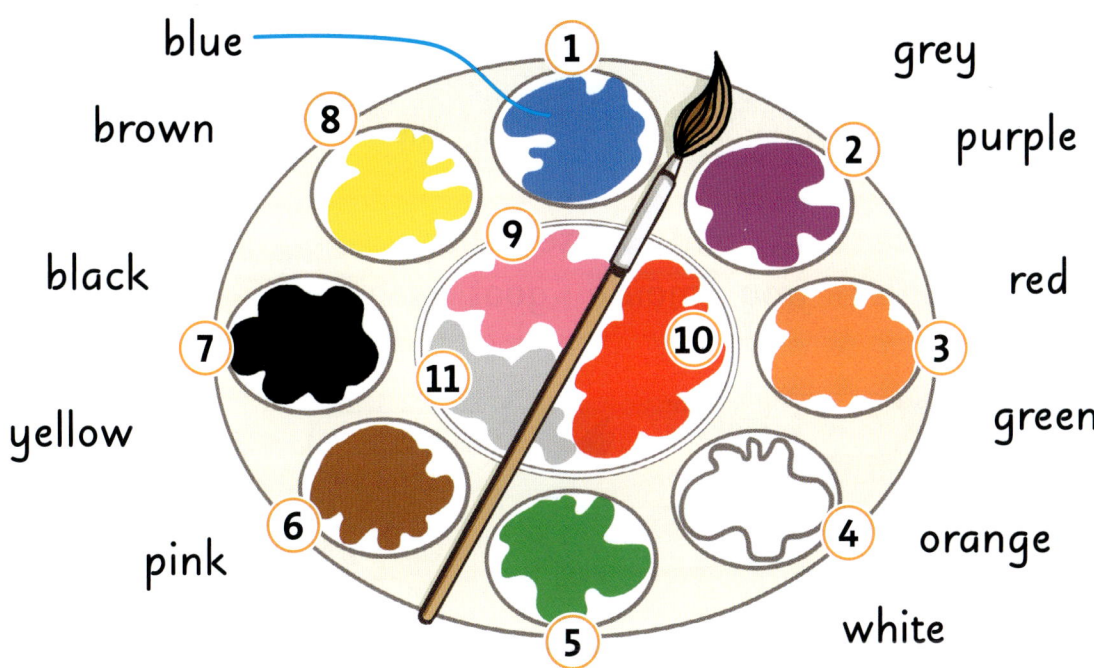

blue
brown
black
yellow
pink

grey
purple
red
green
orange
white

2 Look and write the colours.

1 The elephant is ____grey____ and ____white____.

2 The dog is _____ and _____.

3 The hat is _____ and _____.

4 The apple is _____ and _____.

5 The cat is _____ and _____.

6 The ice cream is _____ and _____.

3 Put six things on your desk. What colour are they? Point and say.

It's red.

It's black.

INTRODUCTION WORDS   see pages 108–109

Hello! unit   **5**

1 I love animals!

Words

1 **Complete the words.**

chicken ~~cat~~ dog bird horse sheep
duck cow fish frog mouse goat bees

Look at the animals!

c _a_ _t_

1 b_____

2 b_____

3 s_____

4 c____

5 h_____

6 g_____

7 d_____

8 c h_____

9 f_____

10 m_____

11 f_____

12 d____

2 **Ask, point and say.**

Where's the frog?

Here's the frog.

3 **Do the speaking activity.** **P** 109

What colour's the horse?

It's brown.

UNIT 1 WORDS   see page 109

Reading & writing

1 **Look at the picture on page 6 and read. Write *yes* or *no*.**

1 The duck is yellow.   __no__
4 The goat is orange.   _____

2 The fish is purple.   _____
5 The bird is red and green.   _____

3 The mouse is grey.   _____
6 The cow is black and white.   _____

2 **Colour and say.**

This bird is blue!

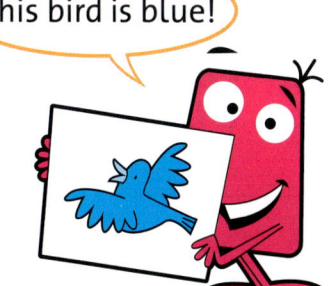

3 **How many are there? Look and write.**

> fish   ~~sheep~~   mouse   mice   donkeys   sheep   fish   donkey

(1)
(2)
(3)
(4)

__one__   __sheep__   _____   _____   _____

(5)
(6)
(7) _____
(8)

_____   _____   _____   _____

Story & writing

1 **Listen and read. Then act.** 🔊 5

2 **Look and write. Listen and check.** 🔊 6

1 Where's Sam?   He's next to the _____dog_____.

2 Where's the frog?   It's on the _____.

3 Where's the mouse?   It's next to the _____.

4 Where's the bird?   It's on the _____.

5 Where's Lucy?   She's in the _____.

Language practice

1 **What animals can you see? Circle the words.**

chicken   mouse

bird

cat   horse

sheep

dog   frog

duck

goat

fish   cow

2 **Read and colour.**

The dogs are brown.

The fish are orange.

The mice are grey.

The horses are pink and blue.

The ducks are yellow and red.

The sheep are purple and green.

Starters practice test

**Look and read. Put a tick (✓) or a cross (✗) in the box.
There are two examples.**

Examples

This is a fish. ✓

This is a cat. ✗

Questions

1

This is a chicken. ☐

2

These are donkeys. ☐

3

This is a horse. ☐

4

These are frogs. ☐

5

This is a sheep. ☐

Starters practice test

Listen and colour. There is one example. 🔊 7

2 At home

Words

1 Ask, point and say.

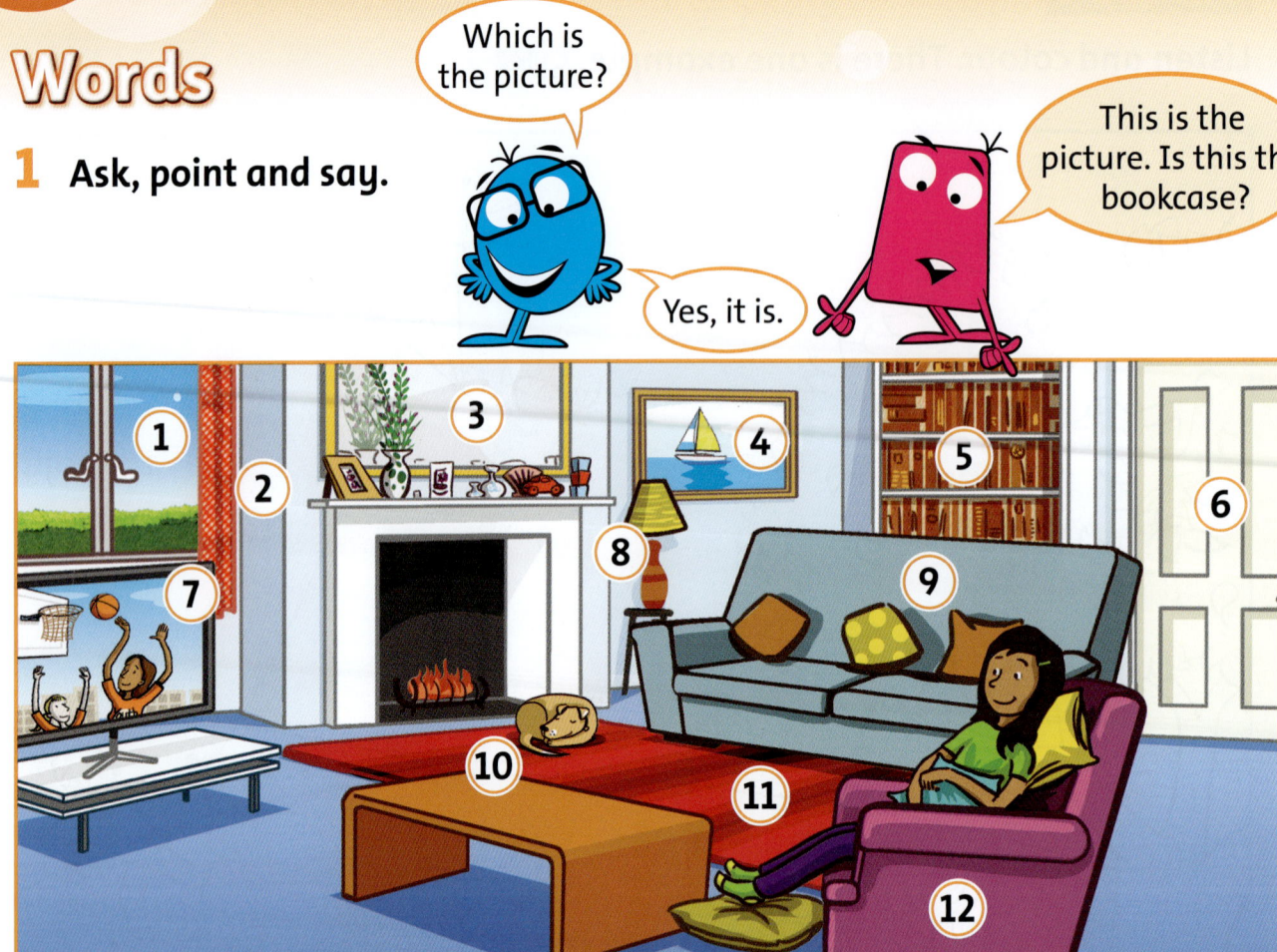

television   rug   window   sofa   lamp   armchair
door   table   bookcase   wall   mirror   picture

2 Look at the picture. Complete the words and write the numbers.

t e l e v i s i o n [7]   s _ f _   [ ]   d _ _ _ _   [ ]

p _ _ _ u _ e [ ]   w _ _ _ _   [ ]   m _ _ _ _ _ r   [ ]

r _ _ _ [ ]   a _ _ c _ a _ _   [ ]   _ a _ p   [ ]

w _ n _ _ w [ ]   t _ _ _ _ _   [ ]   b _ _ _ c _ _ _ _   [ ]

3 Draw and colour a picture of your living room. Talk about it.

Listening & speaking

1 Where's Sam's cat? Look and write.

> behind   between   ~~under~~   in front of

1 It's _____under_____ the bed.

2 It's on the mat _____ the door.

3 It's _____ the sofa.

4 It's _____ the dogs.

2 Listen and draw these things in the picture. 🔊 8

 computer

 clock

 box

 radio

 cupboard

 cat

3 Do the speaking activity. P 110

Where's the computer?

OK. What colour is it?

It's on the desk.

It's blue.

Story & listening

1 **Listen and read. Then act.** 🔊 **9**

2 **Look and complete the words. Listen and draw lines.** 🔊 **10**

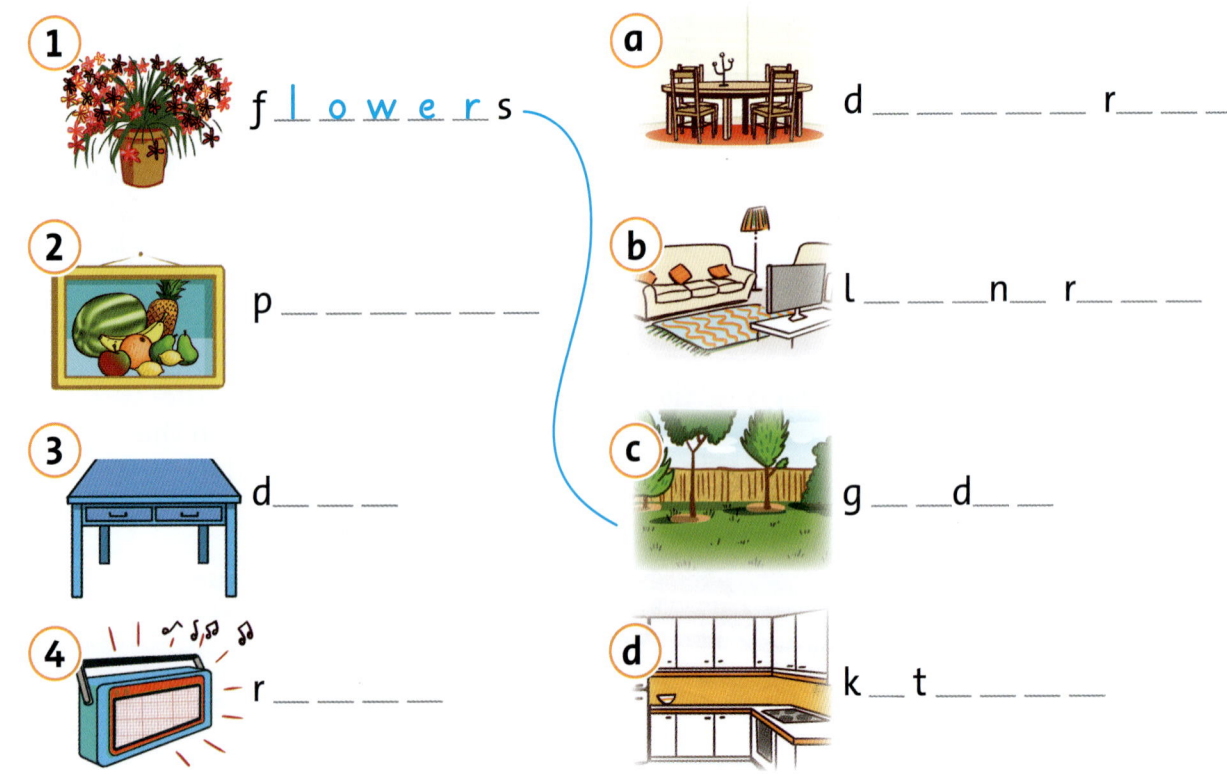

1 f l o w e r s

2 p _ _ _ _ _ _ _

3 d _ _ _ _

4 r _ _ _ _ _

a d _ _ _ _ _ _ _ _ r _ _ _ _

b l _ _ _ n _ r _ _ _ _

c g _ _ d _ _

d k _ t _ _ _ _ _

Language practice

1 **Complete the crossword.**

Starters practice test

Look and read. Write yes or no.

Examples

There's a bird in the tree. _____ yes _____

There's a phone on the table. _____ no _____

Questions

1 There's a clock between the cupboards. _____

2 There's a chair next to the table. _____

3 There's a sheep on the mat. _____

4 There are three frogs in the box. _____

5 There's a cow under the table. _____

Starters practice test

Listen and colour. There is one example. 🔊 11

3 Family and friends

Words

1 Look at the pictures and draw lines.

Sam's mother

Sam's cat

Sam's sister

Sam's father

the baby

boy

Sam

girl

Lucy's mother

Lucy's pet dog

Lucy's grandmother

Lucy's father

Lucy's brother

Lucy's grandfather

Lucy

2 Ask and answer about Sam's family and Lucy's family.

Who's that?

That's Lucy's grandfather.

UNIT 3 WORDS   see pages 109–110

Story & listening

1 **Listen and read. Then act.** 🔊 12

2 **Ask and answer about Lucy.**

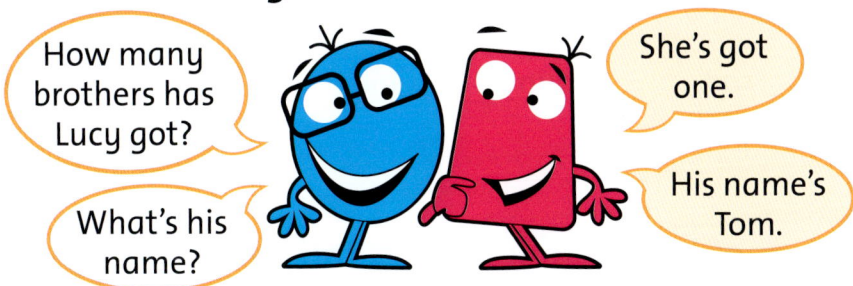

3 **Listen and write a name or a number.** 🔊 13

Sam's got no brothers but he's got
(1) _____two_____ sisters.

(2) _____ is (3) _____ years old.

(4) _____ is a baby.

Sam's got a pet cat. His name's (5) _____.

Reading & speaking

1 **Look and read.**

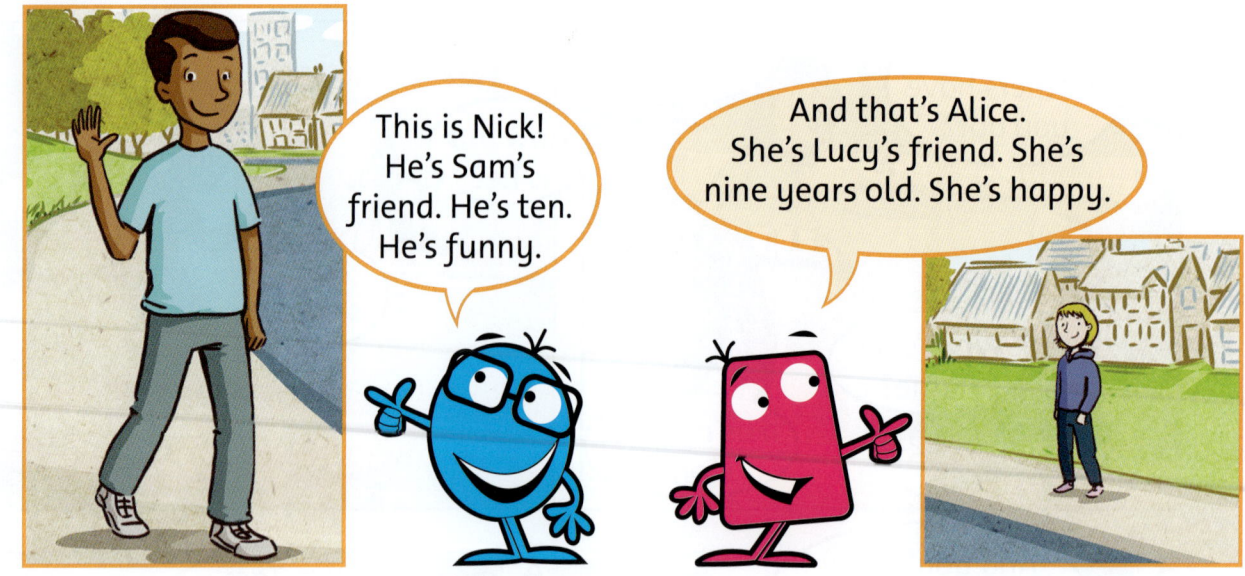

This is Nick! He's Sam's friend. He's ten. He's funny.

And that's Alice. She's Lucy's friend. She's nine years old. She's happy.

2 **Look at the pictures and circle the words.**

1. **big** / small
2. happy / sad
3. old / young
4. small / big
5. sad / happy
6. young / old
7. silly / sad

3 **Draw pictures of two of your friends. Talk about your pictures.**

This is Mark and that's Jill. Mark's ten years old. Jill's funny.

UNIT 3 WORDS   see page 109

Language practice

1 How many of each thing can you find? Count and write your answers.

2 3 4 5 6 7 8 9 10 11 12 13

two clocks	_____ windows	_____ goats
_____ fish	_____ doors	_____ mice
_____ boys	_____ trees	_____ girls
_____ houses	_____ horses	_____ babies

2 Do the speaking activity. **P** 111

What's her name?

Her name's Grace.

Starters practice test

Look at the pictures and read the questions. Write one-word answers.

Examples

Which room is this?　　　　the ____ living room ____

What colour's the sofa?　　　____ purple ____

Questions

1　Who is the boy next to?　　his _____

2　What's on the wall?　　　a _____

3　Where is the mother?　　　_____ the door

4　Which room is this?　　　the _____

5　Who is next to the bed?　　the girl's _____

Starters practice test

Listen and draw lines. There is one example. 🔊14

Kim   Hugo   Eva   Ben

Matt   Sue   Anna

4 Food!

Words

1 Complete the words.

> a banana   an orange   lemons   a pineapple   a mango
> grapes   kiwis   an apple   limes   pears   a watermelon

Look at this fruit!

a b**a n a n a**

2 a p_____

1 an o_____

5 l_____

3 a w_____

4 a m_____

6 p_____

8 g_____

7 k_____

9 l_____

10 an a_____

2 Ask, point and say.

What are these?

They're limes. What's this?

It's a banana.

UNIT 4
WORDS   see page 110

Words & writing

1 Look at this food. Complete the crossword.

bread coconut beans peas rice
potato carrot onion tomato pie

3 →

4 →

6 →

8 →

1 →

2 →

4 →

5 →

6 →

7 →

Crossword:
1 p
2
3 . . . | i
. . . | e
4 5
6 . . . .
7
8 . . . . . .

2 Look and write.

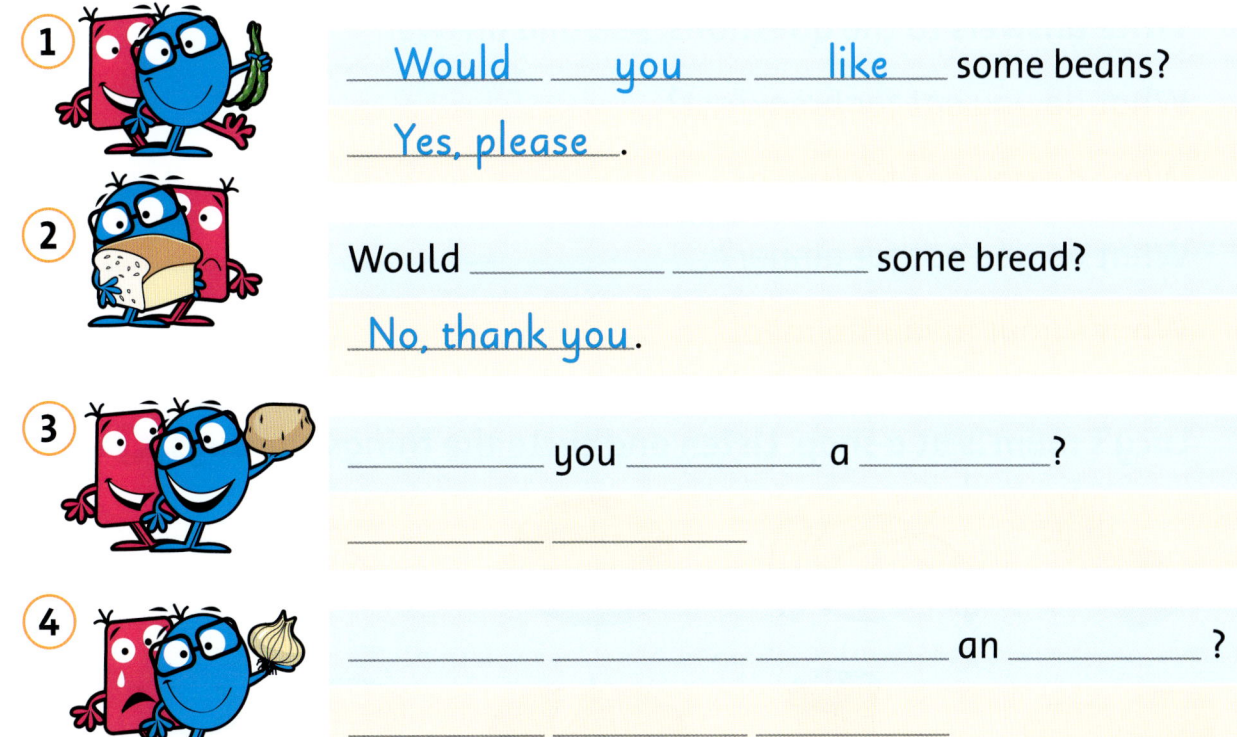

1 __Would__ __you__ __like__ some beans?
   __Yes, please__ .

2 Would _____ _____ some bread?
   __No, thank you__ .

3 _____ you _____ a _____?
   _____ _____

4 _____ _____ _____ an _____?
   _____ _____ _____

Story & listening

1 Listen and read. Then act. 🔊 15

2 Write answers to the questions. Ask and answer.

What do you eat for breakfast? _____

What do you eat for lunch? _____

What do you eat for dinner? _____

What's your favourite meal? _____

3 Lucy's mum is at a shop. Listen and circle the things she buys. 🔊 16

 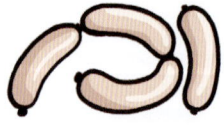  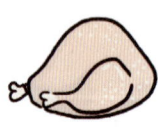 

Language practice

1 **Find ten differences. Talk to your friend about the pictures.**

2 **Do the speaking activity.** P 112

Starters practice test

Look at the pictures. Look at the letters. Write the words.

Example

m e a t b a l l s

Questions

1

_____

2

_____

3

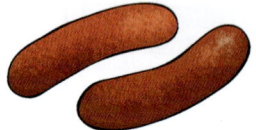

_____

4

_____

5

_____

Starters practice test

Listen and tick (✓) the box. There is one example. 🔊17

Which is Mrs Green?

A  ✓

B

C

1 What's Pat's favourite food?

A

B

C

2 What does Dan eat for breakfast?

A

B

C

3 Where's Sue's phone?

A

B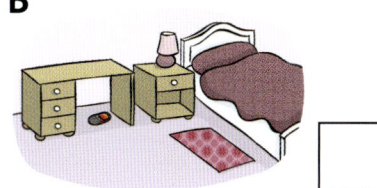

C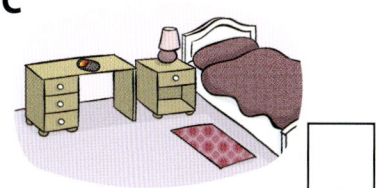

4 Which is Mark's house?

A

B

C

Words

1 Look at the pictures and the letters.
Complete the clothes words in the boxes.

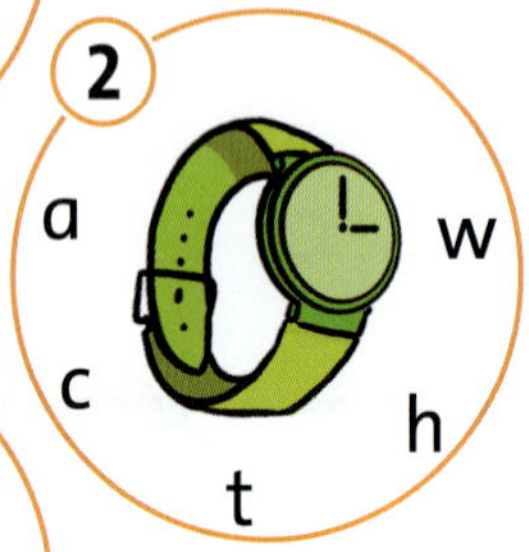

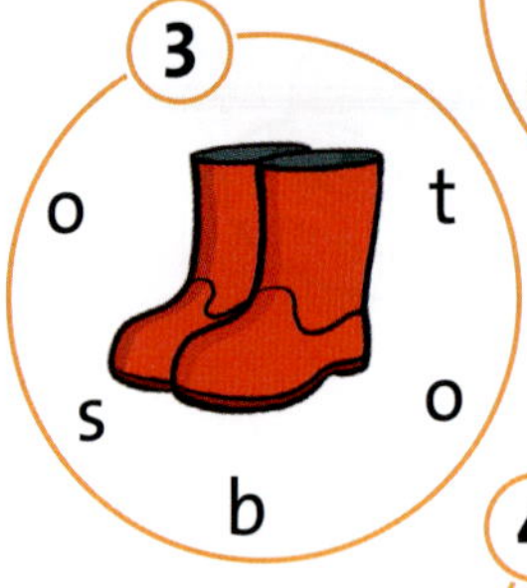

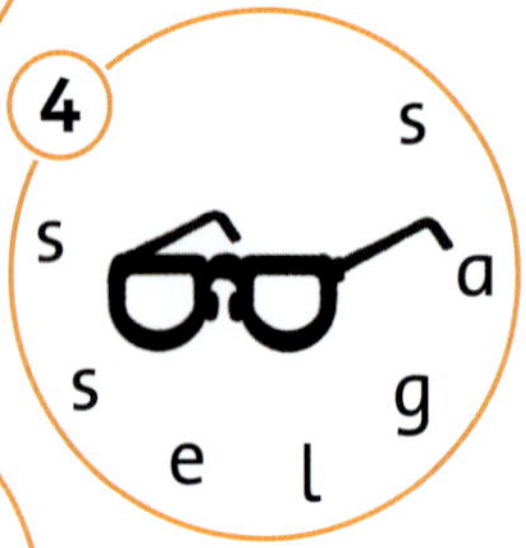

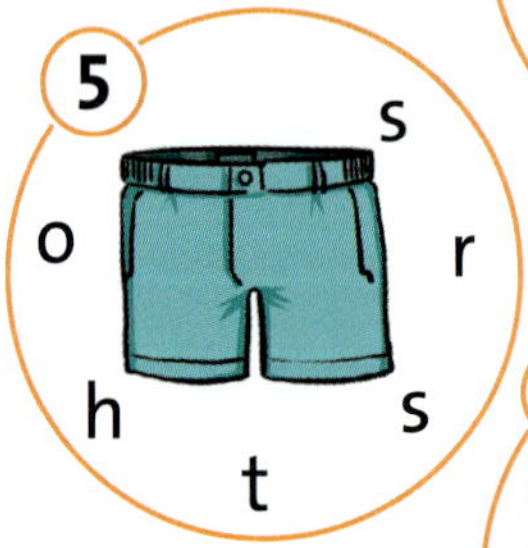

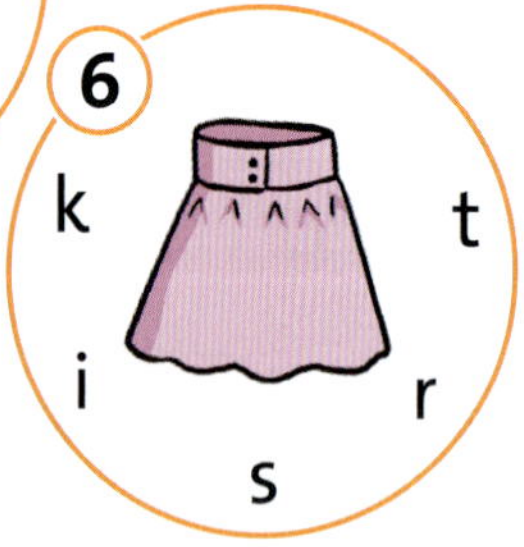

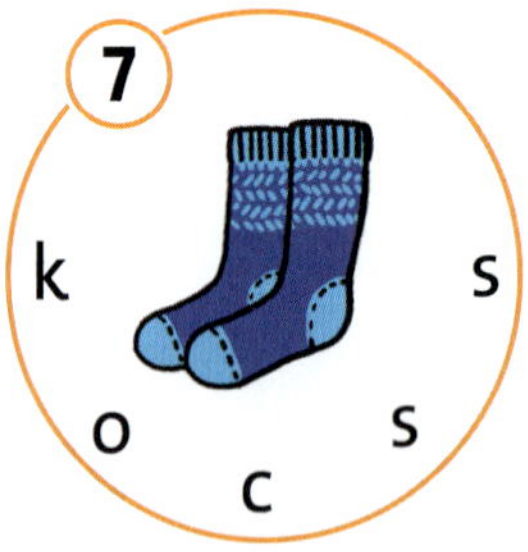

1				
s	h	i	r	t

2			
w	t		

3			
o	t		

4			
l	s		s

5		
s	r	

6			
s	k	t	

7			
s	o	k	

8			
j	c	t	

9		
h	e	

10	
t	

11			
t	o	s	r

12			
T	-	i	t

Picture letter circles:
1. s h t r i
2. a w c h t t
3. o t s o b
4. s a s g e l
5. s r o h s t
6. k t i r s
7. k s o c s
8. k c a e j t
9. e s o h s
10. t h a
11. s e r t u o s
12. t h i s r T -

2 Ask, point and say.

What's this?

They're blue socks.

It's a pink T-shirt. What are these?

UNIT 5
WORDS   see page 110

Speaking & listening

1 **Ask and answer about the clothes in Alice's bedroom.**

> handbag   jeans   T-shirt   hat   dress

dress	
handbag	

Look! It's Alice's bedroom. Where's her dress?

It's on the rug.

Oh dear, where are my things?

2 **Put Nick's clothes in his bedroom. Listen and draw lines.** 🔊 18

Story & listening

1 **Listen and read. Then act.** 🔊19

2 **Say what Lucy and Alice are wearing.**

3 **What is Sam wearing? Listen and colour.** 🔊20

4 **Write about what you're wearing.**

What are you wearing today?
I'm wearing _____

_____

_____

_____ .

Language practice

1 Look at the pictures. Find and circle the eleven words and write them in the word groups.

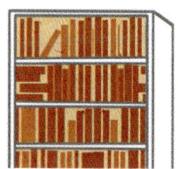

q	b	r	o	t	h	e	r	q	r
w	p	o	q	g	r	e	y	w	e
e	a	f	o	l	l	a	h	e	h
l	s	a	q	k	n	j	k	m	t
r	t	g	p	c	c	j	r	o	o
t	i	i	i	v	m	a	l	u	m
y	e	h	n	b	g	c	s	s	k
u	i	j	k	w	h	k	l	e	d
i	p	k	x	s	s	e	r	d	r
o	d	l	m	e	a	t	l	f	j

Food	Things in the house	Animals	Clothes	Family	Colours
pie					

2 Do the speaking activity. **P** 113

She's wearing a pink skirt and a red hat.

Starters practice test

Read this. Choose a word from the box. Write the correct word next to numbers 1–5. There is one example.

Houses

Some houses have got four windows and a ＿＿＿＿＿ _door_ ＿＿＿＿＿. You can sit on the **(1)** ＿＿＿＿＿＿＿＿＿＿ in the living room and listen to things on the **(2)** ＿＿＿＿＿＿＿＿＿＿. You can cook meals in the **(3)** ＿＿＿＿＿＿＿＿＿＿ then eat with the family in the dining room. At night you go to sleep in a bedroom. The child's bedroom in this house is blue. There's a bed, a **(4)** ＿＿＿＿＿＿＿＿＿＿ with a computer on it, and a cupboard with lots of **(5)** ＿＿＿＿＿＿＿＿＿＿ in it, too.

example

door   clothes   kitchen   poster

radio   pets   desk   sofa

Starters practice test

Read the question. Listen and write a name or a number.
There are two examples. 🔊 21

Examples

What's the girl's name? _____ Eva _____

How old is she? _____ 12 _____

Questions

1 What is the number of Eva's house? _____

2 What is Eva's friend's name? _____

3 How many animals has Eva got? _____

4 What is the name of Eva's pet dog? _____

5 How old is Eva's dog? _____

Revision 1

1 Look at the picture for one minute.
Listen to your teacher and write the answers.

2 Look at the pictures. Do the crossword.

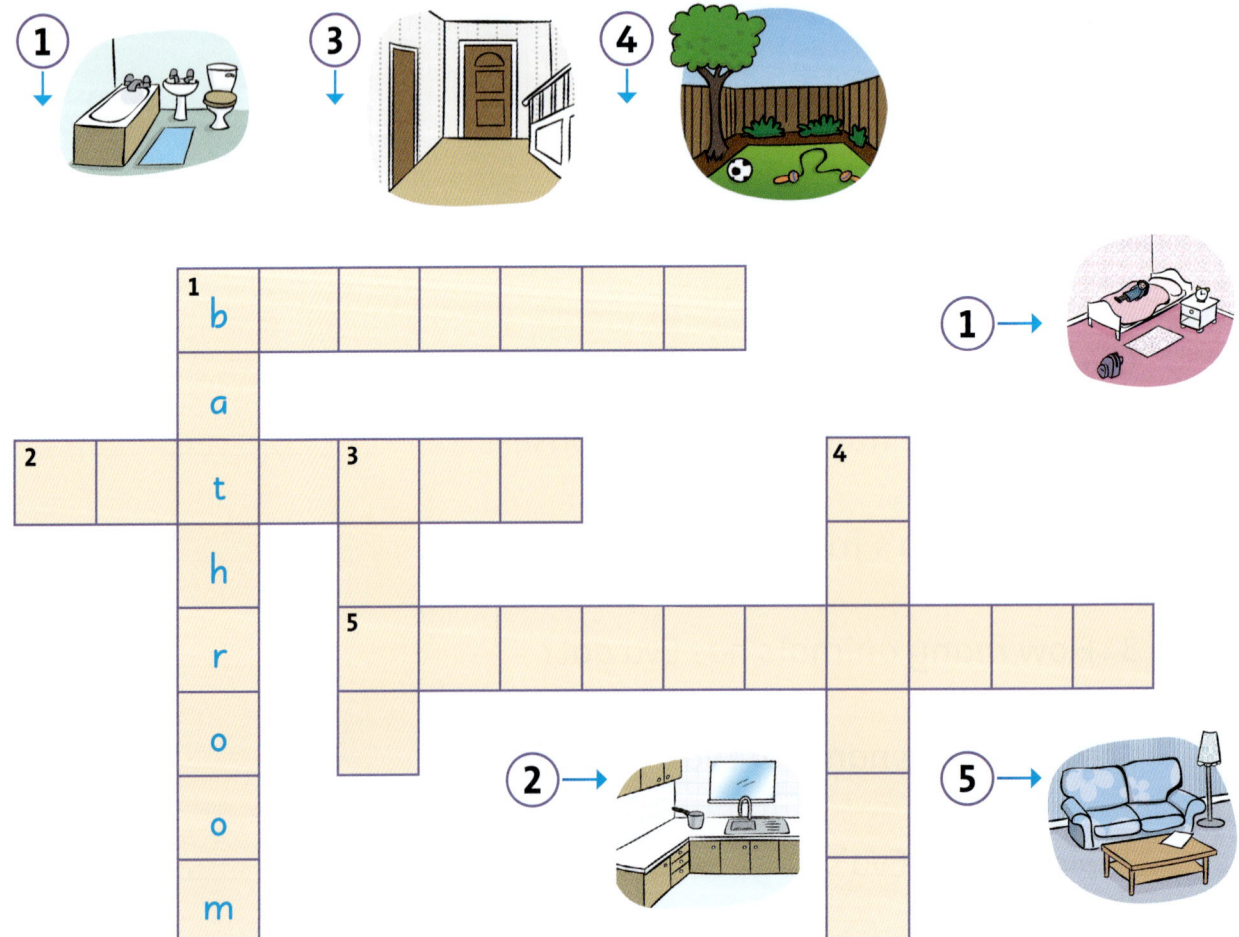

**REVISION 1
WORDS**   see pages 108 – 110

3 **Find ten differences. Talk to your friend about the pictures.**

4 **What's in Sue's bag? Listen and draw lines.** 🔊22

5 Look at the picture. Write the words.

How quickly can you write the words? Write the times.

Start time: _____   End time: _____

1 f <u>l o w e r s</u>	11 s ___ ___ ___ ___
2 w ___ ___ ___	12 s ___ ___ ___
3 d ___ ___ ___	13 c ___ ___ ___ ___
4 d ___ ___	14 s ___ ___ ___ ___
5 l ___ ___ ___ ___	15 T- ___ ___ ___ ___
6 m ___ ___ ___ ___ ___	16 t ___ ___ ___ ___ ___ ___ ___
7 b ___ ___ ___ ___ ___ ___	17 m ___ ___
8 t ___ ___ ___ ___	18 b ___ ___ ___
9 f ___ ___ ___ ___	19 s ___ ___ ___ ___
10 d ___ ___ ___	20 h ___ ___ ___ ___ ___ ___

1 **Look at the picture in Activity 2. Write sentences about where to put these things.**

> in   on   next to   under   in front of   behind   between

Student A

orange   <u>Put the orange</u> _____

grapes   _____

sausages   _____

onion   _____

Student B

mango   <u>Put the mango</u> _____

banana   _____

lime   _____

coconut   _____

2 **Tell your friend where to put the things. Listen and draw lines.**

3 **Tell your friends about:**

- your house
- your favourite food
- your family

6 Look at us!

Words

1 **Complete the words.**

> body mouth feet ear arm eye face
> leg tail hair hand foot nose ~~head~~

Hi! Look at me. I'm an alien!

h e a d

1 ___ y ___

2 ___ ___ r

3 ___ ___ u ___ ___

4 a ___ ___ ___

5 ___ ___ ___ y

6 t ___ ___ ___ ___

7 f ___ ___ ___ ___

8 h ___ ___ ___ ___

9 ___ ___ ___ n ___

10 ___ ___ a ___ ___ ___

11 n ___ ___ ___ ___

12 ___ e ___

13 ___ ___ ___ e ___

2 **Do the speaking activity.** P 114

My alien has got one mouth.

My alien has got two mouths!

UNIT 6 **WORDS** see pages 110–111

Story & writing

1 **Listen and read. Then act.** 🔊 23

2 **Look at the story and read the questions. Write one-word answers.**

1 How many children are there in this story? _____ *four*

2 What are Nick and Alice doing in picture 1? playing a _____

3 What colour is Lucy's favourite doll's dress? _____

4 What colour is Lucy's favourite doll's hair? _____

5 What is Nick wearing? a T-shirt and _____

6 What does Lucy like playing? _____

3 **Choose a person in your family. Write about his/her hair and his/her eyes.**

My _____ has got _____
_____ hair and _____ eyes.

1 Sam and Lucy are talking about the toys. Listen and draw lines. 🔊24

elephant   spider

frog

Look at us!
We're toys.

alien

robot

tiger

kite

duck

snake

monkey   doll   monster

2 Which toy don't they talk about? Write about that toy.

It's a _____ . It's _____

and it's got _____ .

3 Ask and answer.

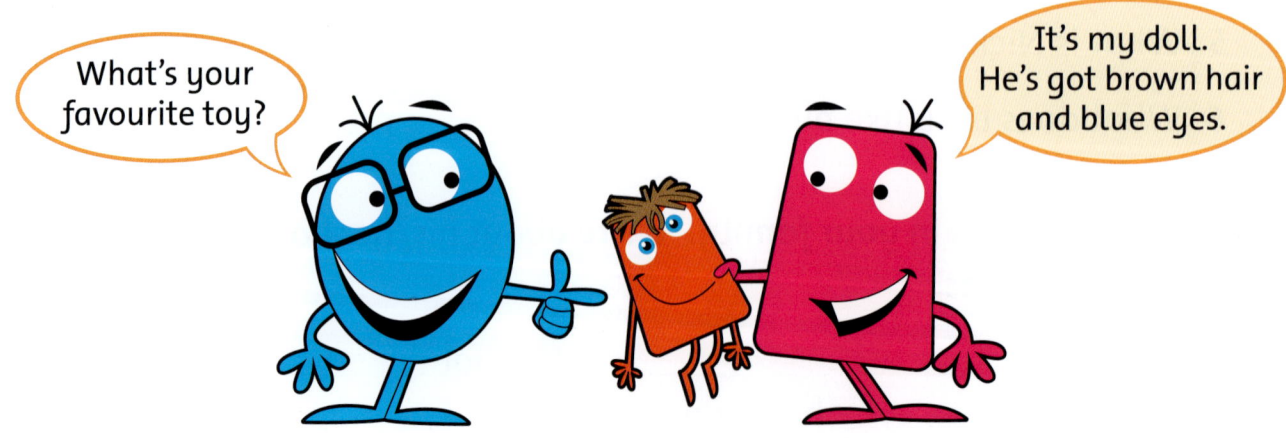

What's your
favourite toy?

It's my doll.
He's got brown hair
and blue eyes.

Language practice

1 **Look and write the words.**

1. t e d d y
   b e a r

2. _ _ _

3. _ _ _

4. _ _ _ _ _ _ _ _

5. _ _ _

6. _ _ _ _ _ _

7. _ _ _ _ _ _

8. _ _ _

9. _ _ _ _ _

10. _ _ _ _

2 **Write the words.**

an	a
elephant	teddy bear
arm	leg

3 **Write the words.**

body	toys
a leg	a teddy bear
an arm	an elephant

4 **Find the children's toys. Listen and write *L* for Lucy, *S* for Sam, *A* for Alice and *N* for Nick.** 🔊25

1. ☐ L   ☐
2. ☐   ☐
3. ☐   ☐
4. ☐   ☐

Starters practice test

Look and read. Write yes or no. There are two examples.

Examples

There are three birds sitting in a tree. _____yes_____

The girl is happy. _____no_____

Questions

1 The boy is standing in front of the elephant. _____

2 The monkey is holding a pear. _____

3 The girl has got long brown hair. _____

4 The monkey is standing behind the tree. _____

5 The girl is wearing a pink T-shirt. _____

Starters practice test

Listen and tick (✓) the box. There is one example. 26

Which is Bill's favourite toy?

A

B

C  ✓

1 Which is Anna's father?

A

B

C

2 What's May's sister wearing?

A

B

C

3 What does Mark want to eat?

A

B

C

4 What's Alex doing?

A

B

C

7 We love school!

Words

1 Look and write the numbers next to the words.

> Look at our classroom!

book	5	computer		mouse	
teacher		board		rubber	
ruler		keyboard		page	
pen		poster		pencil	
painting		crayon		paper	

2 Complete the sentences.

> in front of   on   next to   under

1 There is a rubber _____ the mat.

2 There are some pencils _____ the chair.

3 The teacher is _____ the board.

4 The mouse is _____ the keyboard.

UNIT 7 WORDS   see page 111

Speaking & reading

1 Ask and answer questions about the picture on page 46. Write.

> ruler   pen   picture   bag   book   banana

Who's holding a ruler?

Bill.

Who's picking up a pencil? _____

2 Look and read.

There are **a lot of** rubbers on this desk! And there are **some** pencils.

Yes, and there are **lots of** rulers in this bag!

3 Read, draw and colour.

1 Draw **a lot of** pens and crayons in the bag. Colour **some** crayons blue and **some** crayons pink. Colour the pens orange.

2 Write **lots of** letters and **some** numbers on the board.

3 Draw **lots of** rulers and rubbers on the desk. Colour **some** rulers green, **some** orange and **one** yellow. Don't colour the rubbers!

Story & reading

1 **Listen and read. Then act.** 🔊27

1

Hi Jill. Are you OK?

Yes, Mum.

2

What are you doing?

Oh, good!

I'm making dinner and Sam is learning his words for an English test.

3

And the baby?

She's sleeping!

4

Oh no!

Well done! I'm coming home now, Jill!

2 **Read and write *yes* or *no*.**

1   Two girls are writing. _yes_

2   The teacher is showing a picture. _____

3   Two girls are standing up. _____

4   One child is pointing at a man. _____

5   A girl is picking up a pen. _____

6   Five children are sitting down. _____

7   Two boys are talking. _____

8   The man is smiling at the teacher. _____

Language practice

1 **Look at the pictures. Write the words in the crossword.**

3 letters

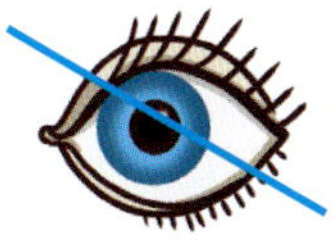

4 letters

1 c			p			2

3 | 4 e | | |
y
e

5

6

7

8

9

10

11

12

5 letters

13

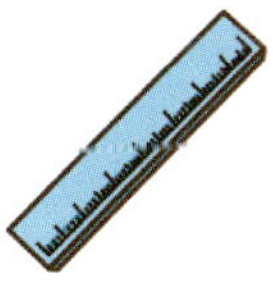

6 letters

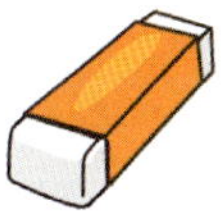

7 letters

8 letters

2 **Do the speaking activity.** P 115

What's she doing?

She's picking up a book.

Starters practice test

Look and read. Put a tick (✓) or a cross (✗) in the box.
There are two examples.

Examples

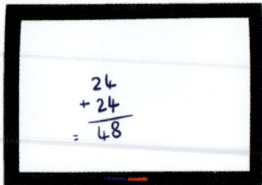

This is a board. ✓

This is a kiwi. ✗

Questions

1

These are pies.

2

This is a frog.

3

These are lamps.

4

This is a leg.

5

These are tigers.

Starters practice test

Listen and draw lines. There is one example. 🔊28

Anna   Matt   Grace   Alex

Pat   Eva   Hugo

(8) In the playground

Words

1 Find six sports and colour them. Use different colours.

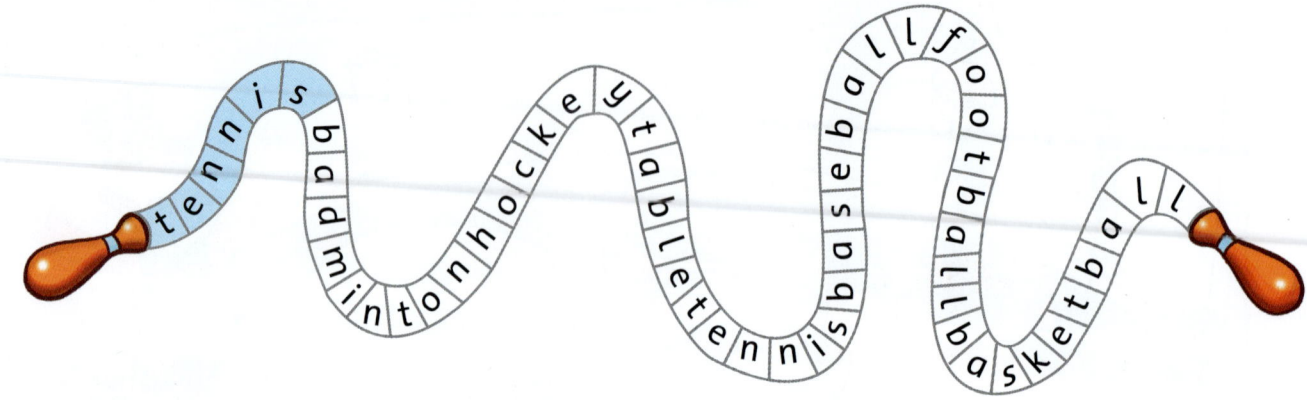

2 Write the sports from Activity 1 under the pictures.

1 _basketball_   2 _____   3 _____   4 _____

5 _____   6 _____   7 _____

3 Ask and answer.

Can you play tennis?

Yes, I can!

No, I can't. Can you?

UNIT 8 WORDS   see page 111

Listening & speaking

1 **Listen and draw lines.** 🔊 29

① ② ③

④ ⑤ ⑥

⑦ ⑧ ⑨

May

Alex

Tom

Pat

Grace

Ben

Dan

2 **Do the speaking activity.** 🅿 116

Story & writing

1 Listen and read. Then act.

2 Look and complete the sentences.

running ~~kicking~~ hitting riding walking bouncing

1 Two boys are playing football. Sam is _____kicking_____ the ball.

2 Lucy is playing tennis. She is _____ the ball.

3 One boy is _____ his bike.

4 One girl is _____ to the playground.

5 One girl is _____ with a ball, and she's _____ it.

UNIT 8
WORDS   see page 111

Language practice

1 Find ten differences. Talk to your friend about the pictures.

2 Write the things from the picture in Activity 1.

1

lita

_____tail_____

2

erpa

_____

3

catwh

_____

4

rdpise

_____

5

nchcike

_____

6

ckyheo

_____

Starters practice test

Look at the pictures and read the questions. Write one-word answers.

Examples

How many trees are there?   _____ two _____

What's the man holding?   a _____ bag _____

Questions

1 Where's the girl?   _____ her mum

2 What's the woman wearing?   a blue _____

3 Which animal is the boy pointing at?   the _____

4 What's the mouse doing?   _____

5 Which animal is running?   the _____

Starters practice test

Listen and tick (✓) the box. There is one example. 🔊31

What's Kim taking to school?

A

B  ✓

C

1 Where's Ben's dad?

A

B

C

2 What's Mark's favourite sport?

A

B

C

3 Which is Grace's new toy?

A

B

C

4 What does Alex want for dinner?

A

B

C

9 My hobbies

Words

1 Look and draw lines to find the hobbies in the pictures.

1	playing	pictures
2	painting and drawing	in the park
3	doing	stories
4	flying	with Dad
5	singing	board games
6	making	in the sea
7	listening	the piano or guitar
8	reading	cakes
9	fishing	songs
10	running and jumping	sport
11	swimming	to music
12	playing	a kite

2 Ask and answer.

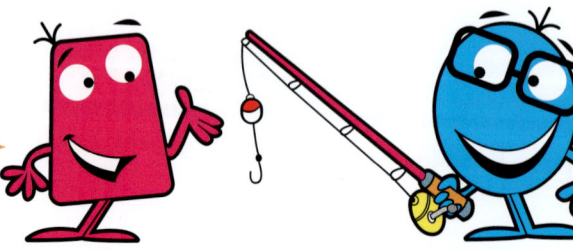

What's your favourite hobby?

I like fishing.

UNIT 9 WORDS   see page 111

Story & writing

1 **Listen and read. Then act.** 🔊32

2 **Read and write *your* answers.**

I love flying kites!

I like making cakes!

I enjoy painting pictures.

I like playing the piano.

I love playing basketball.

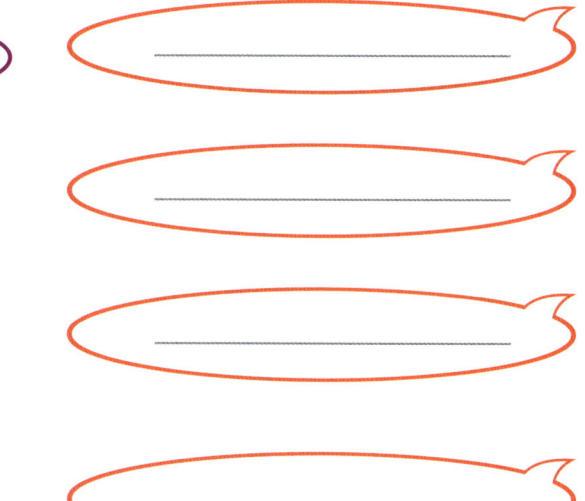

Listening & speaking

1 **Listen and draw lines.** 🔊 33

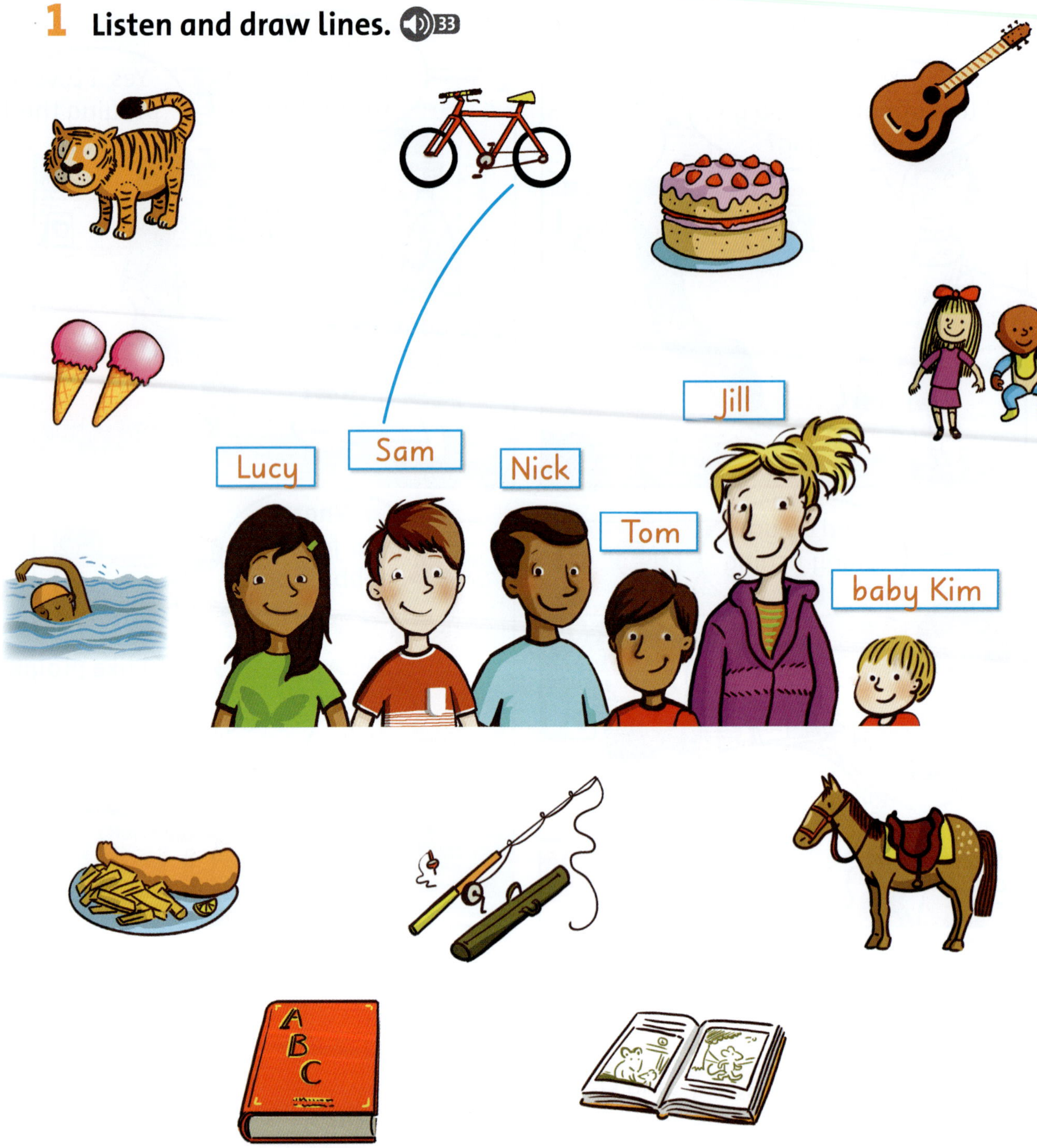

Lucy   Sam   Nick   Tom   Jill   baby Kim

2 **Do the speaking activity.** P 117

I like playing tennis.

So do I.

Language practice

1 **Find the things that Bill and Sue like in the picture. Write.**

Bill

Bill likes things starting with the letter **B**.

Sue likes things starting with the letter **S**.

Sue

How many things does Bill like? _____

How many things does Sue like? _____

2 **Spell the things that Sue likes and the things that Bill likes. Listen and check.** 🔊34

Sue likes _sausages_ , _____

_____ .

Bill likes _balls_ , _____

_____ .

Starters practice test

Reading & Writing, Part 4

Read this. Choose a word from the box. Write the correct word next to numbers 1–5. There is one example.

Sports and hobbies

There are some great sports for kids. You can go to the ___park___

and play (**1**) _____ or football. You can also go

(**2**) _____ in the sea. There are lots of fun hobbies,

too. You can sit in the garden and draw (**3**) _____ of

the flowers and animals there. Some children like to play the

(**4**) _____ or the piano. When you're at home, play

some (**5**) _____ with your family. It's a cool thing to do!

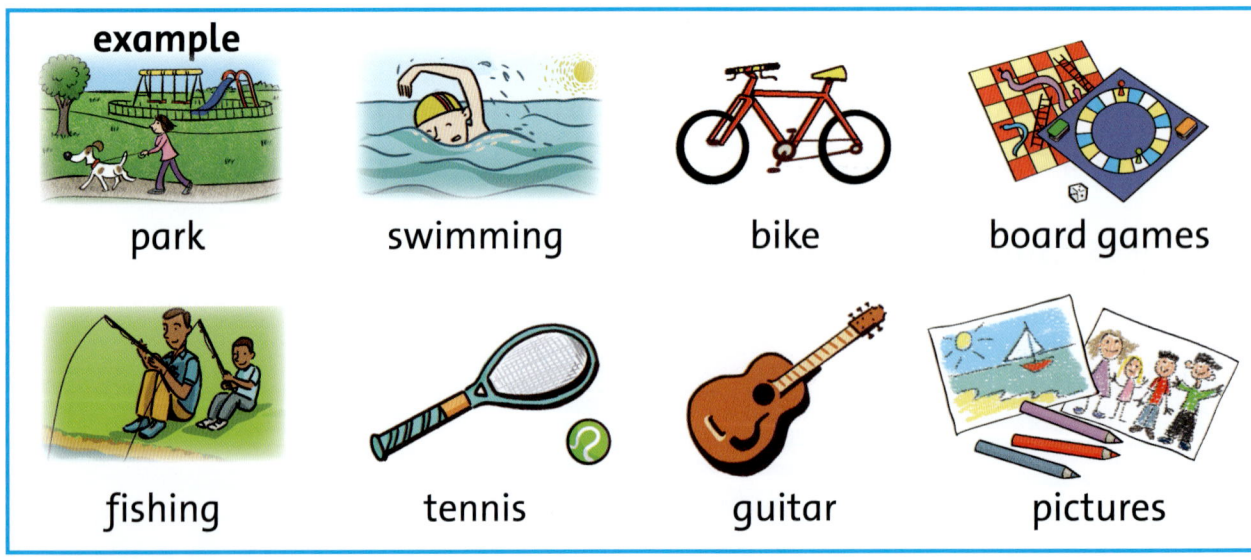

example			
park	swimming	bike	board games
fishing	tennis	guitar	pictures

Starters practice test

Read the question. Listen and write a name or a number. There are two examples. 🔊35

Examples

What's the boy's name? _____ Ben _____

How old is he? _____ 7 _____

Questions

1 What's Ben's mother's name? _____

2 What's Ben's sister's name? _____

3 How many robots has Ben got? _____

4 What's the name of Ben's friend? _____

5 How old is Ben's friend? _____

10 Your day

Words

1 Look at the letters. Write the words under the pictures.

ebd	latofobl	ivetlesnio	nindre	okob

airdo	selsnos	sarbekfat	rapk	hoslco

1 b e d

2 _____

3 _____

4 _____

5 _____

6 _____

7 _____

8 _____

9 _____

10 _____

2 Draw lines and make five sentences about you.

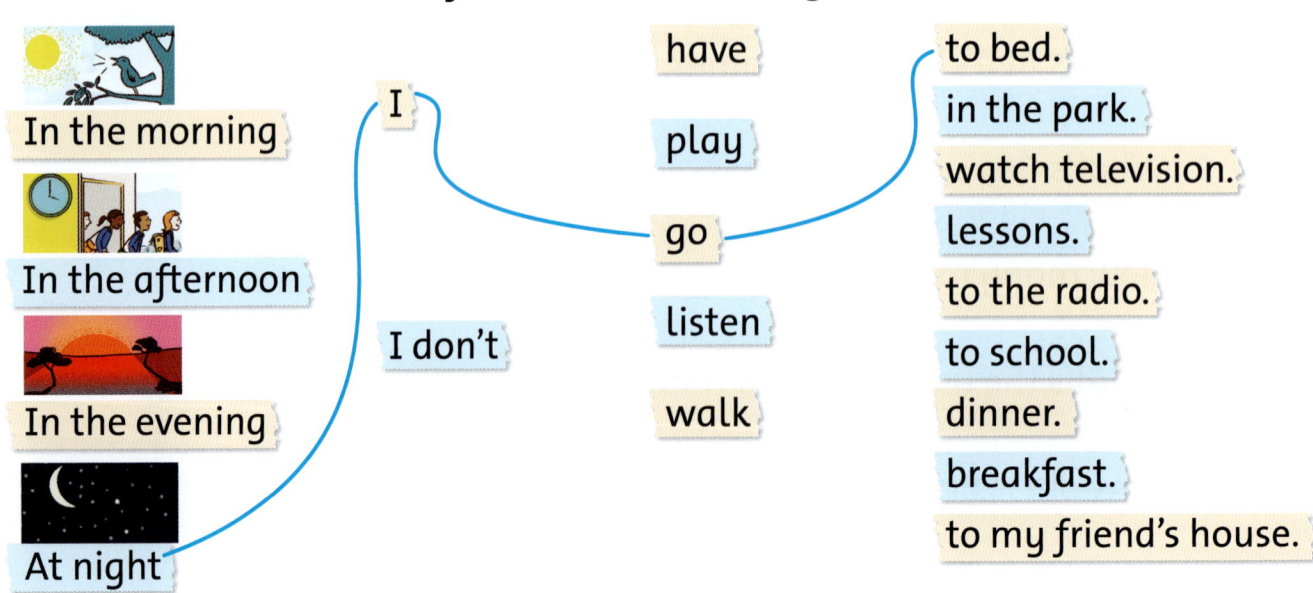

In the morning

In the afternoon

In the evening

At night

I

I don't

have

play

go

listen

walk

to bed.

in the park.

watch television.

lessons.

to the radio.

to school.

dinner.

breakfast.

to my friend's house.

UNIT 10 **WORDS** see page 112

Story & speaking

1 Listen and read. Then act. 🔊 36

1 What do you do in the morning?

I have breakfast and I play football.

2 Do you play in the park in the afternoon?

Yes, I do! I play football again in the afternoon.

3 What do you do in the evening?

I have dinner and I watch football on TV.

4 Do you listen to the radio at night?

No, I don't. I read stories about football!

2 Write about your day.

In the morning I _____.

In the afternoon I _____.

In the evening I _____.
I don't _____.

At night I _____.

3 Do the speaking activity. P 118

In the morning, Bill has breakfast with his family.

Listening

1 Lucy is talking about what she does in the morning. Listen and write numbers in the boxes. 🔊37

1

2 Sam is talking about what he does in the afternoon and evening. Listen and tick (✓) or cross (✗). 🔊38

①  ✓  ✗

②

③

④

⑤

⑥

Language practice

1 **What are these stories about? Write the first letter of each word in the pictures and find the answers.**

1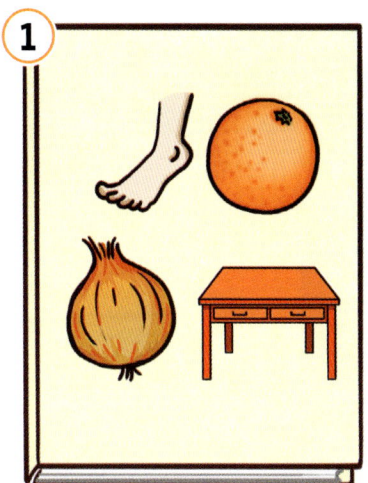

It's about
eating
<u>f o o d</u>.

2

It's about
playing
__ __ __ __.

3

It's about
__ __ __ __.

4

It's about
going to
__ __ __ __ __.

5

It's about
riding
__ __ __ __ __.

6

It's about
__ __ __ __ __ __.

2 **Read. Tell your friend about the stories you read.**

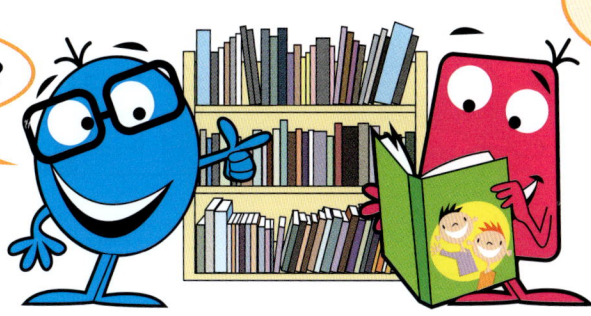

Do you read stories?

Yes, I do. I'm reading a story about making friends now.

Starters practice test

Read this. Choose a word from the box. Write the correct word next to numbers 1–5. There is one example.

A School Day

In the morning, children get up and have ___breakfast___. At school, they have lessons with their teacher and the other children in their (1) _____. Some children play sport or have music lessons. In the evening, many children go (2) _____ and have dinner with their (3) _____. They do their school work, watch TV or play games. They wash in the (4) _____, put on their night clothes and go to bed. Then they go to (5) _____. It's a long day.

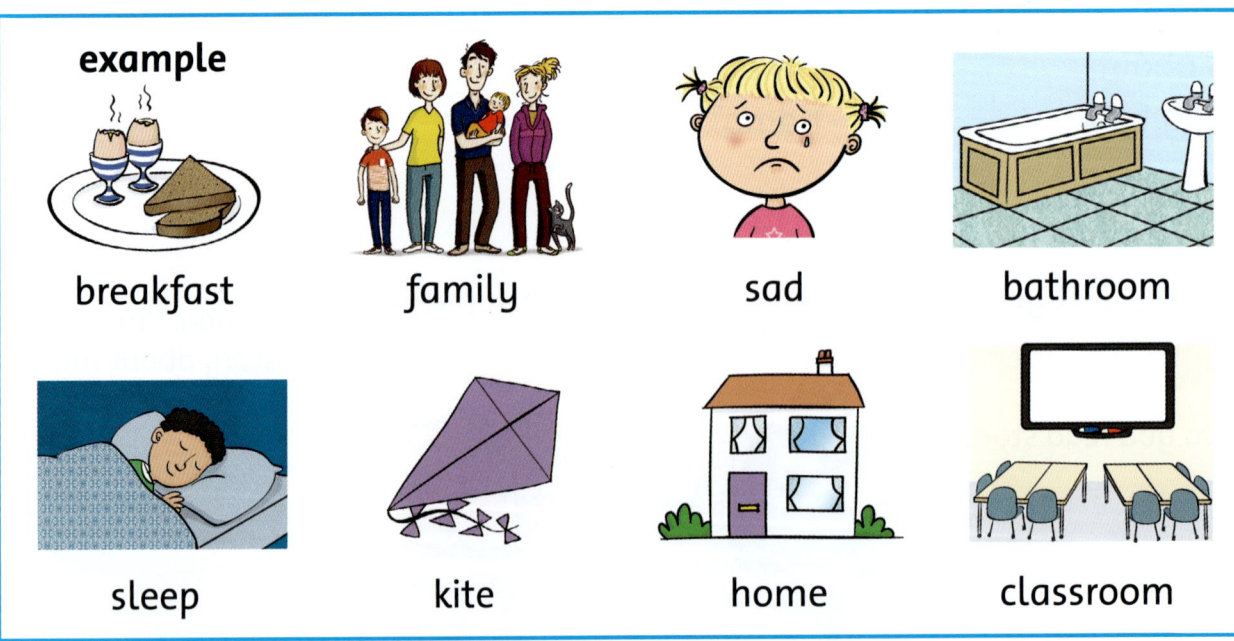

example			
breakfast	family	sad	bathroom
sleep	kite	home	classroom

Starters practice test

Listen and colour. There is one example. 🔊 39

Revision 2

1 **Read and colour the monster.**

face – blue

mouth – red

feet – grey

eyes – orange

hands – brown

ears – pink

nose – black

hair – yellow

legs – green

body – purple
and pink

2 **How many things can you find in the picture? Write the words.**

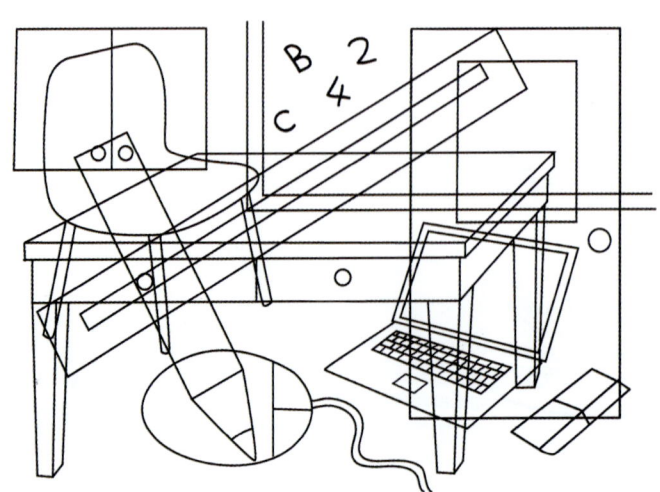

_____

_____

_____

_____

_____

_____

_____

3 Grace is at school with her mother. She's talking about the children. Listen and draw lines. 🔊40

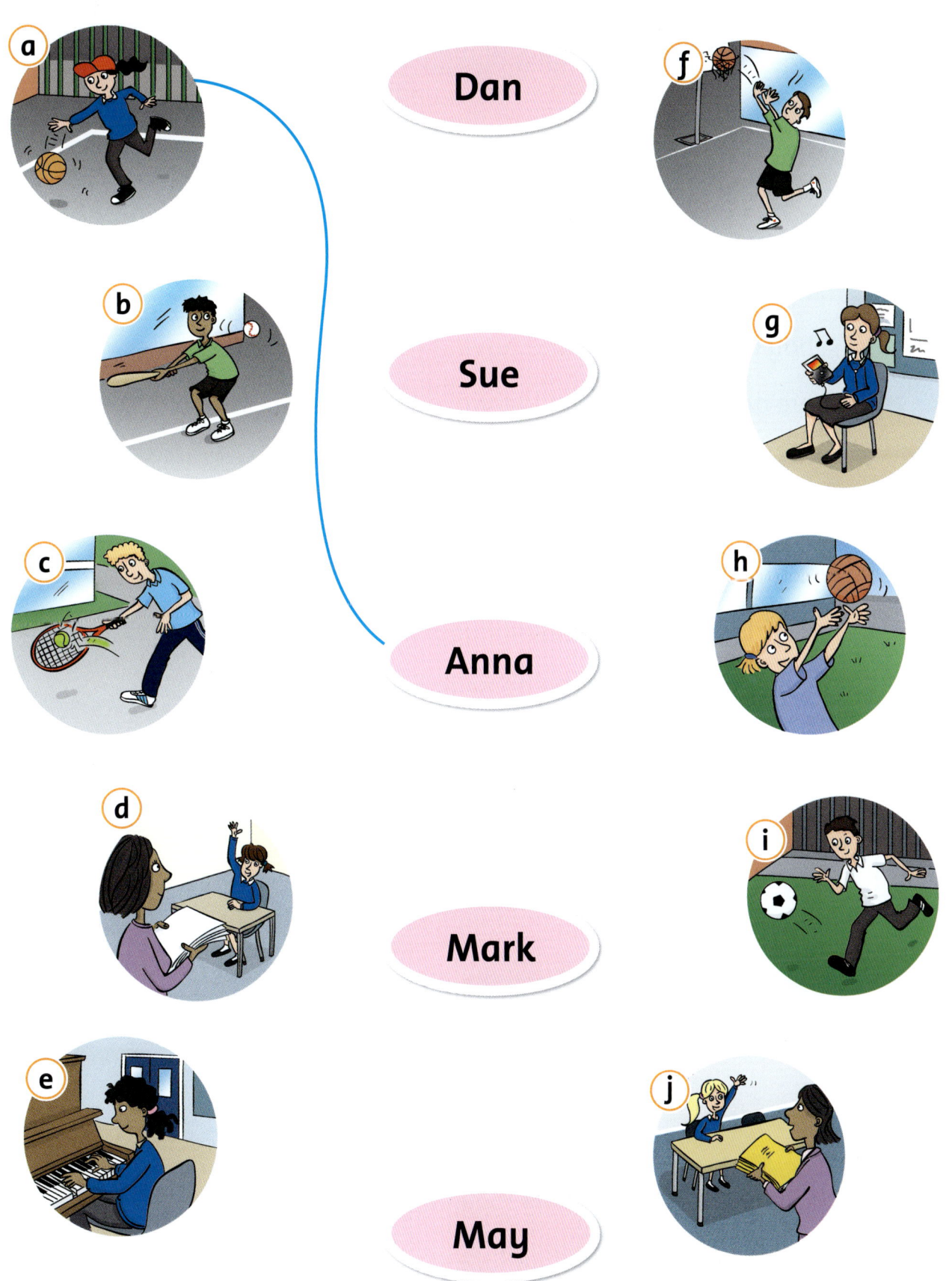

Dan

Sue

Anna

Mark

May

4 **Look and read. Write *yes* or *no*.**

1   A boy is riding a bike and having fun. _____yes_____

2   There are three ducks in the water. _____no_____

3   A girl is doing a painting. _____

4   Two boys are fishing under a tree. _____

5   Two girls are playing badminton. _____

6   Two girls are flying kites. _____

7   The boy who's riding the horse is waving. _____

5 **Write the words.**

> kicking   throwing   catching   standing
> ~~riding~~   bouncing   sitting   jumping

①    **②**    **③**    **④**

_____riding_____   _____   _____   _____

⑤    **⑥**    **⑦**    **⑧**

_____   _____   _____   _____

1 **Look at the picture. Ask and answer these questions.**

Student A

1 What are the children doing?

2 What's in the box?

3 How many snakes can you see?

Student B

1 What colour eyes has the boy got?

2 Is the girl smiling?

3 Where's the monster?

2 **Ask your teacher for the object cards. Take turns to tell your friend where to put things.**

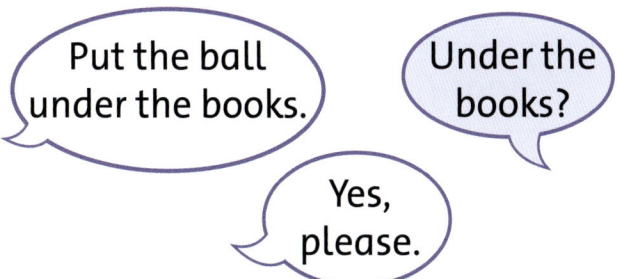

Put the ball under the books.

Under the books?

Yes, please.

3 **Now tell your friend about the people in your family.**

- What colour is their hair?
- What colour are their eyes?
- What do they like doing?
- What sports can they play?

My dad's got black hair.

My mum can play tennis.

11 In the street

Words

1 Look and write the numbers next to the words.

a motorbike	8	a bus		a lorry	
a car		a train		a ship	
a helicopter		a bike		a plane	

2 Write the words.

~~open~~   new   closed   angry

1 open   2 _____   3 _____   4 _____

UNIT 11 WORDS   see page 112

Words & writing

1 **Look at the picture on page 74 again. Draw lines and make sentences.**

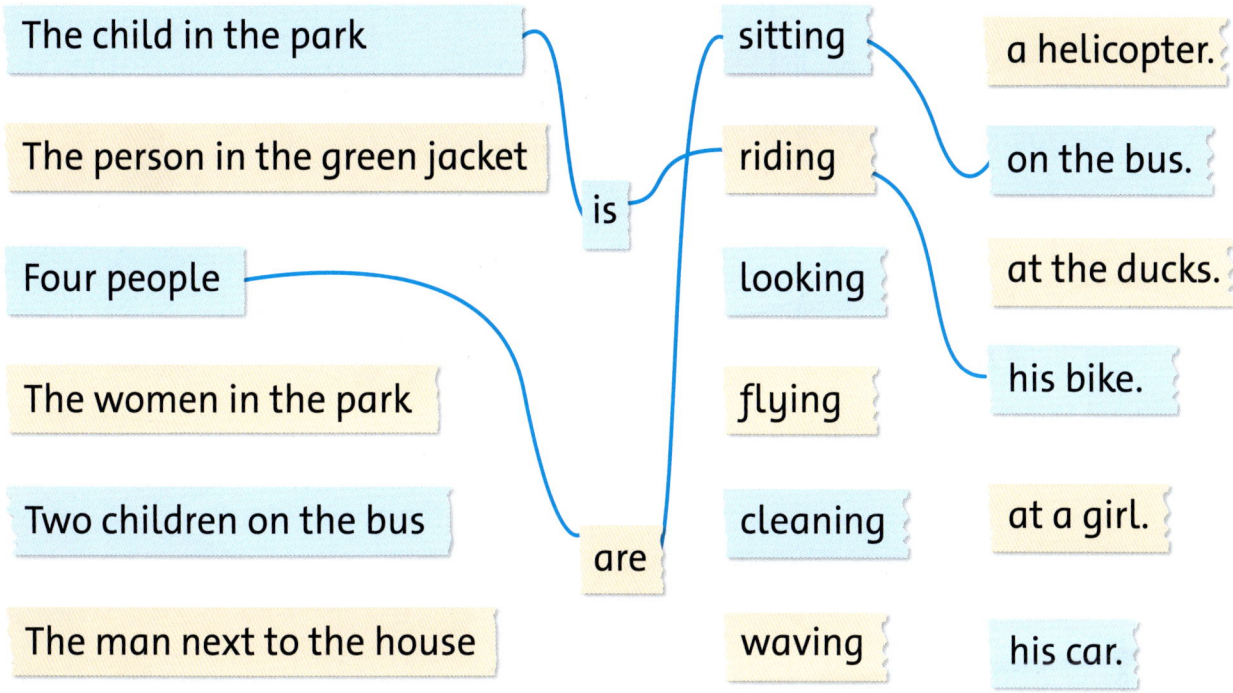

The child in the park

The person in the green jacket

Four people

The women in the park

Two children on the bus

The man next to the house

is

are

sitting

riding

looking

flying

cleaning

waving

a helicopter.

on the bus.

at the ducks.

his bike.

at a girl.

his car.

2 **Circle and write about what you're doing with your friends in class today.**

My class is a **big / small** class. There are _____ children in my

class. There are _____ girls and _____ boys. We've

got a fantastic teacher. **Her / His** name's **Mrs / Mr** _____. Today

we're learning about _____. Some children are

_____, one boy is _____

and one girl is_____. We aren't

_____ in class today.

UNIT 11 WORDS   see page 112

Story & listening

1 Listen and read. Then act. 🔊 41

2 Listen to Lucy and tick (✓) or cross (✗). 🔊 42

1

 ✓

 ✗

2

 ☐

 ☐

3

 ☐

 ☐

4

 ☐

 ☐

Language practice

1 Colour the lines from the pictures to the words.

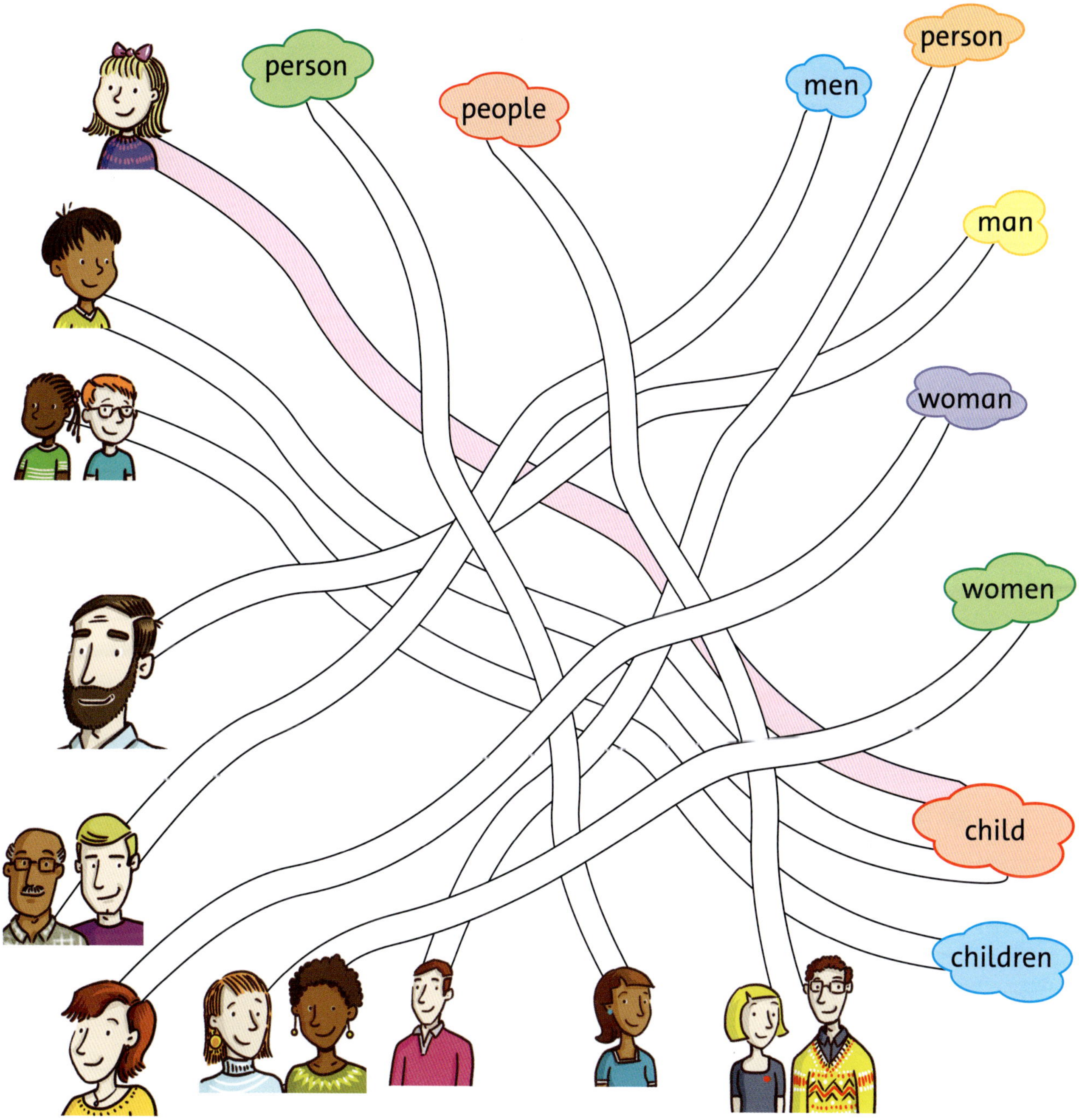

person

people

men

person

man

woman

women

child

children

2 Do the speaking activity. **P** 119

Where's the cat?

It's on the house.

Starters practice test

Reading & Writing, Part 3

Look at the pictures. Look at the letters. Write the words. There is one example.

Example

 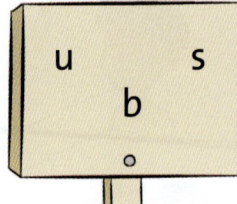

b u s

Questions

1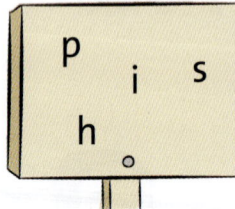

_ _ _ _

2

_ _ _ _ _

3

_ _ _ _ _

4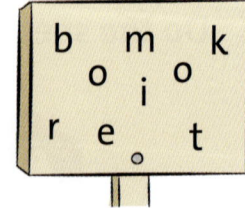

_ _ _ _ _ _ _ _

5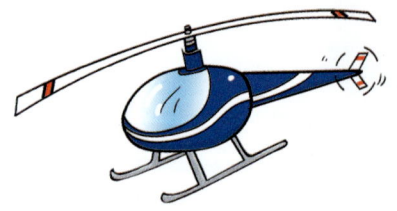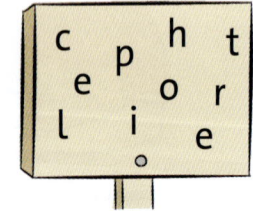

_ _ _ _ _ _ _ _ _ _

Starters practice test

Listen and draw lines. There is one example. 🔊43

Jill   Pat   Dan   Eva

Hugo   May   Matt

12 My grandparents

Words

1 Sam is seeing his grandparents today. Look at the picture and write the words in the boxes.

| boat / car | trousers / jacket / dress | sheep / horses |
| house / flat | ~~in~~ / next to / on | mother / sister / father |

Sam and Jill are [in] the [ ] with their [ ]

and [ ] and their baby [ ], Kim. They're waving at their

grandparents. Their grandfather's wearing a blue [ ] and brown

[ ]. Their grandmother's wearing a yellow [ ]. Sam and

Jill's grandparents don't live in a [ ]. They live in a [ ].

It's [ ] a park. In the park there are some animals. There are

two [ ] and three [ ]. Today there's a [ ]

[ ] the water.

Speaking & words

1 **Listen and read. Then act.** 🔊44

2 **Draw lines from the words to their opposites.**

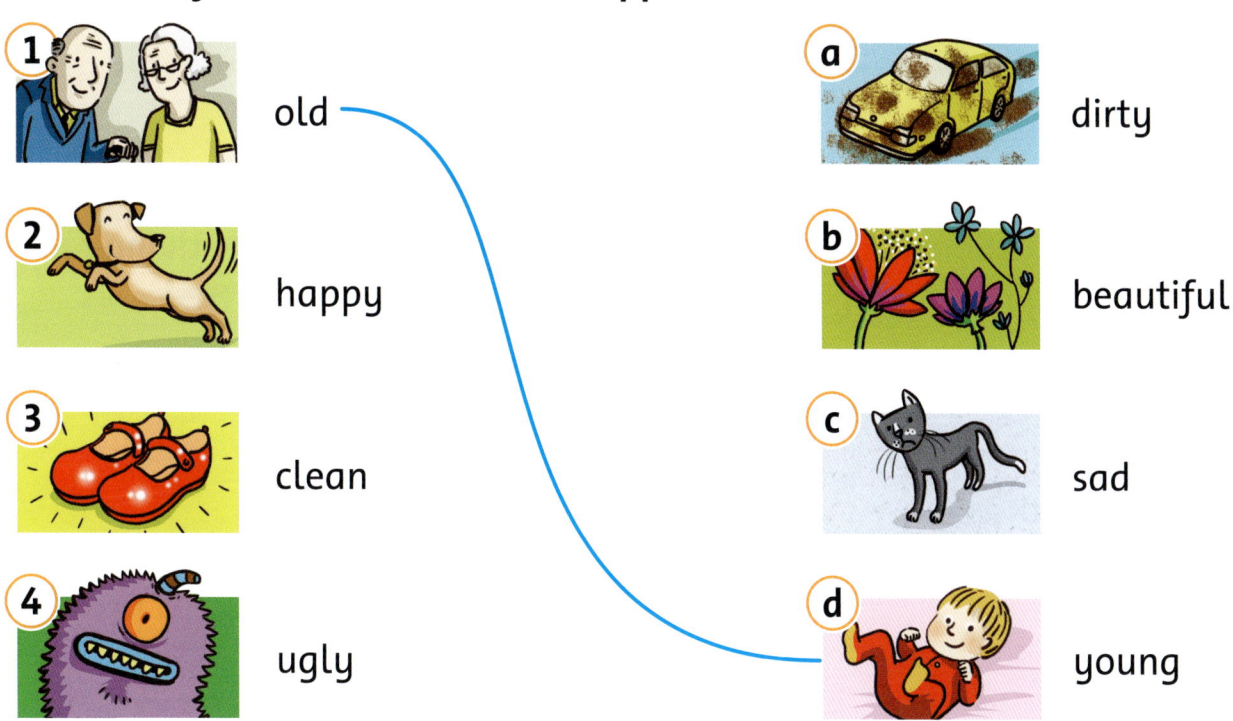

Story & writing

1 **Ask and answer about Sam's family.**

2 **Look at the picture and complete the words.**

In the kitchen	In the dining room	In the living room
c u p b o a r d s	p _ _ t _ _ e	a _ _ c _ _ _ _ r
d _ _ _ _	t _ b _ _ _	l _ _ _ _
w _ _ d _ _	c _ _ i _ s	m _ _ _ _ _ r
c _ _ _ k	b _ _ g _ _ s	p _ _ _ e
_ _ d _ o	c _ i _ _ r _ n	t _ _ _ _ v _ s _ _ n

Language practice

1 **Listen to Lucy. Circle the correct pictures.** 🔊 45

A    B    C

A    B    C

A    B    C

A    B    C

A    B    C

2 **Do the speaking activity.** P 120

I've got some brown trousers.

Reading & Writing, Part 2

Look and read. Write **yes** or **no**. There are two examples.

Examples

The family is in the garden.	yes
Mum is pointing at the cat.	no

Questions

1 The dog has got a sausage. _____

2 Grandpa is reading a book. _____

3 The baby is taking some sweets. _____

4 Grandma is smiling. _____

5 There's a helicopter between
the sun and the house. _____

Starters practice test

Listen and tick (✓) the box. There is one example. 🔊46

Which is Ben's grandfather?

A  ✓

B  ☐

C  ☐

1 Which is Mr Green's car?

A  ☐

B  ☐

C  ☐

2 Which is Grace's favourite fruit?

A  ☐

B  ☐

C  ☐

3 What sport does Dan like playing?

A  ☐

B  ☐

C  ☐

4 How does May go to school?

A  ☐

B  ☐

C  ☐

13 Going to the zoo

Words

1 Complete the animal words. Listen and number. 🔊47

p __ __ a __ b __ a __   z __ __ __ __ __

c _r_ o _c_ o _d_ i _l_ e   t __ __ __ __   s __ __ __ __

m __ __ __ __ __   b __ __ __   g __ r __ f __ e

h __ p __ o   l __ z __ __ d   e __ __ __ __ __ __ __

2 Which animal don't the children talk about?

_____

Words & writing

1 **Match the pictures and words. Say.**

 zoo

school

home

 park

shops

see / a polar bear   choose / shoes   write / stories   have / a bath
ride / a bike   fly / a kite   buy / a book   take / photos   eat / lunch

You can write stories at school.

And you can ride a bike at the park.

2 **Read and write answers.**

1   Would you like to go to the zoo? <u>Yes, I want to see the polar bears.</u>

2   Would you like to go to the shops? _____

3   Would you like to go home? _____

4   Would you like to go to the park? _____

Story & speaking

1 Listen and read. Then act. 🔊48

2 Look and say.

drinking   eating   ~~sleeping~~
swimming

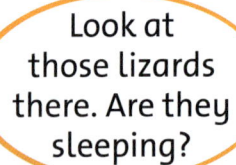

UNIT 13 WORDS see page 112

Language practice

1 **Write the answers to find the animal.**

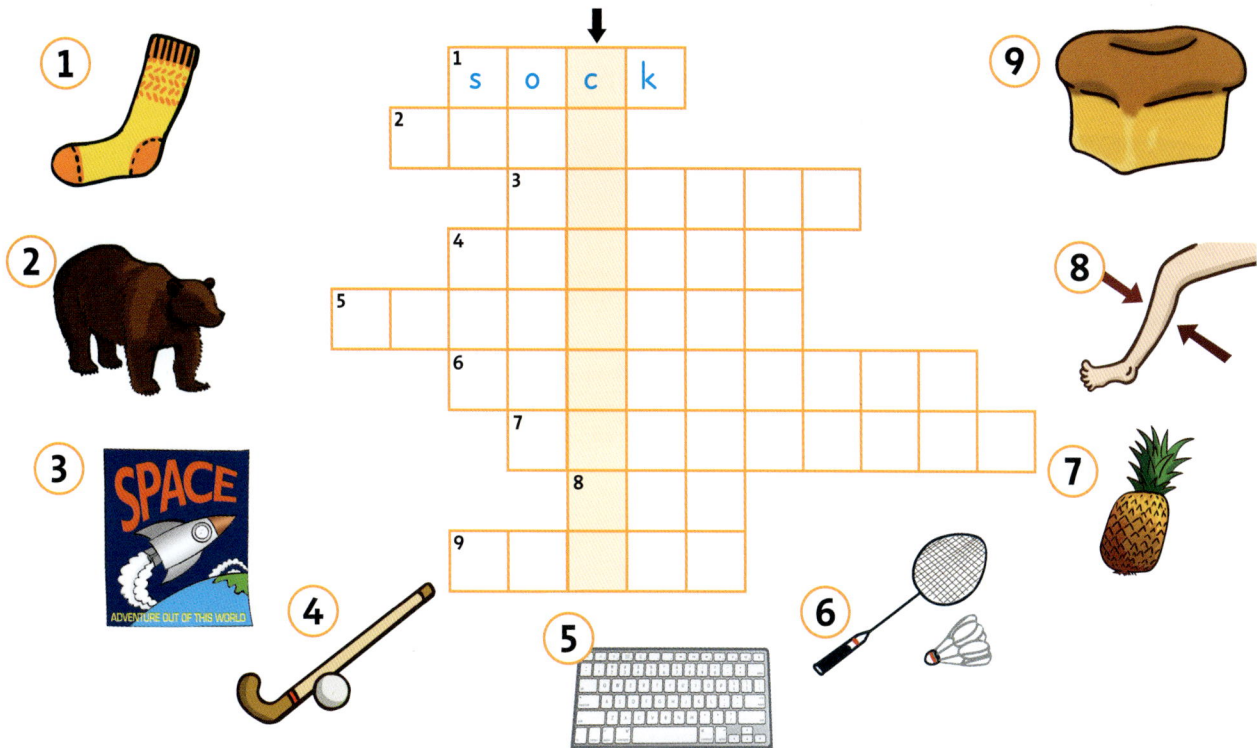

Crossword:
1. s o c k

2 **Find the animals.**

t	c	l	h	p	c	i	d	z	f
i	o	g	i	r	a	f	f	e	l
g	w	z	p	z	t	c	b	b	r
e	l	e	p	h	a	n	t	r	e
r	r	d	o	l	j	r	h	a	d
m	o	n	k	e	y	m	d	h	i
e	q	f	i	s	h	e	b	m	p
c	r	o	c	o	d	i	l	e	s

3 **Do the speaking activity.** **P** 121

Would you like to read a book?

Yes.

Starters practice test

Look at the pictures and read the questions. Write one-word answers.

Examples

Where's the bird?　　　　　　　　next to the _____ sun _____

How many giraffes are there?　　　　_____ two _____

Questions

1　What colour is the girl's handbag?　　_____

2　Where's the baby giraffe?　　　　　　_____

　　　　　　　　　　　　　　　　　　its mother

3　How many flowers are there?　　　　_____

4　Which animal is on the hippo?　　the _____

5　What colour is the lizard?　　　　　_____

Starters practice test

Listen and colour. There is one example. 🔊49

14 Happy birthday!

Words

1 Complete the words.

1 c <u>a m e r a</u>

2 w _ _ _ _ _

3 t _ _ _ _ _ _

4 b _ _ _ _ _ _ _ _

5 s _ _ _ _ _ _ _ _ _

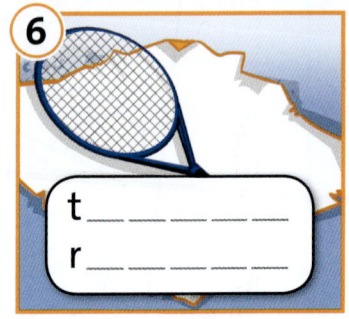
6 t _ _ _ _ _ _
r _ _ _ _ _ _

7 b _ _ _ _

8 c _ _ _ _ _ _ _ _ _ _

9 l _ _ _ _ _ _

2 Listen and write the numbers of the presents next to the names. 🔊50

Lucy	2
Grandpa	
Jill	
Sam	
Mum and Dad	
Matt	

Hugo	
Grandma	
Dad	

The presents are for Tom, but who are they from?

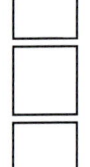

UNIT 14 WORDS   see page 112

Words

1 Here are some drinks for Tom's party. Match the words with the pictures.

milk   lemonade   water   orange juice

2 Read this with your friend. Say words where there are pictures.

It's Tom's party this afternoon. Hooray! His mum's in the 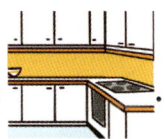.

She's making a fantastic birthday  for Tom. Look! Tom's in the

. There are  on the  and lots of  too!

3 Talk about the picture.

Story & writing

1 **Listen and read. Then act.** 🔊51

2 **Look at the pictures and write.**

~~mine~~   theirs   hers   ours   his

1  Whose are these sweets? They're _____ mine _____.

2  Whose is this robot? It's _____.

3  Whose is this doll? It's _____.

4 Whose are these games? They're _____.

5  Whose is this kite? It's _____.

①

②

③

④

⑤

Language practice

1 Write the first letter of each word to find the message.

c ___ ___ ___

___ ___ ___

___ ___ ___ ___ ___ ___ ___

___ ___ ___ ___ ___

2 Do the speaking activity. **P** 122

I've got the balloons.

**Look at the pictures. Look at the letters. Write the words.
There is one example.**

Example

_c a k e_

Questions

1

____ ____ ____ ____ ____

2

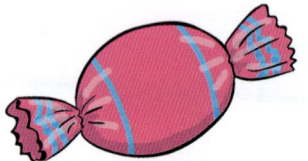

____ ____ ____ ____ ____

3

____ ____ ____ ____ ____ ____

4

____ ____ ____ ____ ____ ____

5

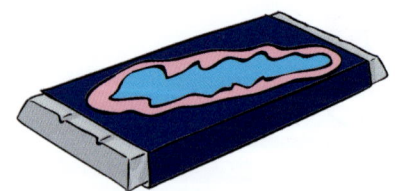

____ ____ ____ ____ ____ ____ ____

Starters practice test

Read the question. Listen and write a name or a number. There are two examples. 🔊52

Examples

What's the girl's name? _____ Anna _____

What is the number of her house? _____ 16 _____

Questions

1 How many presents has Anna got today? _____

2 What's the name of her favourite toy? _____

3 How many people are there in her family? _____

4 What's her brother's name? _____

5 How old is Anna today? _____

15 At the beach

Words

It's a beautiful day. We're at the beach! What can you see on the beach and in the sea?

1 Draw lines from the words to the pictures.

sea sand beach water jellyfish shells

2 Can you find these things in the picture? Complete the words.

b a d m i n t o n
k _ _ _ e
b _ _ l _

i _ _ _ c r _ _ _ m
b _ na _ _ _ s
l _ _ _ _ n _ d _

_ _ s _
_ i _ e
b _ _ a _

d _ _ _ s _
t _ _ u _ e _ _ _
h _ _ _ _ b _ _ _

Words & listening

1 Draw lines from the pictures to the words.

to drink
to kick
to wear
to eat
to fly
to read
to ride
to listen to

2 What are the children doing on the beach this morning?
Listen and draw lines. 🔊53

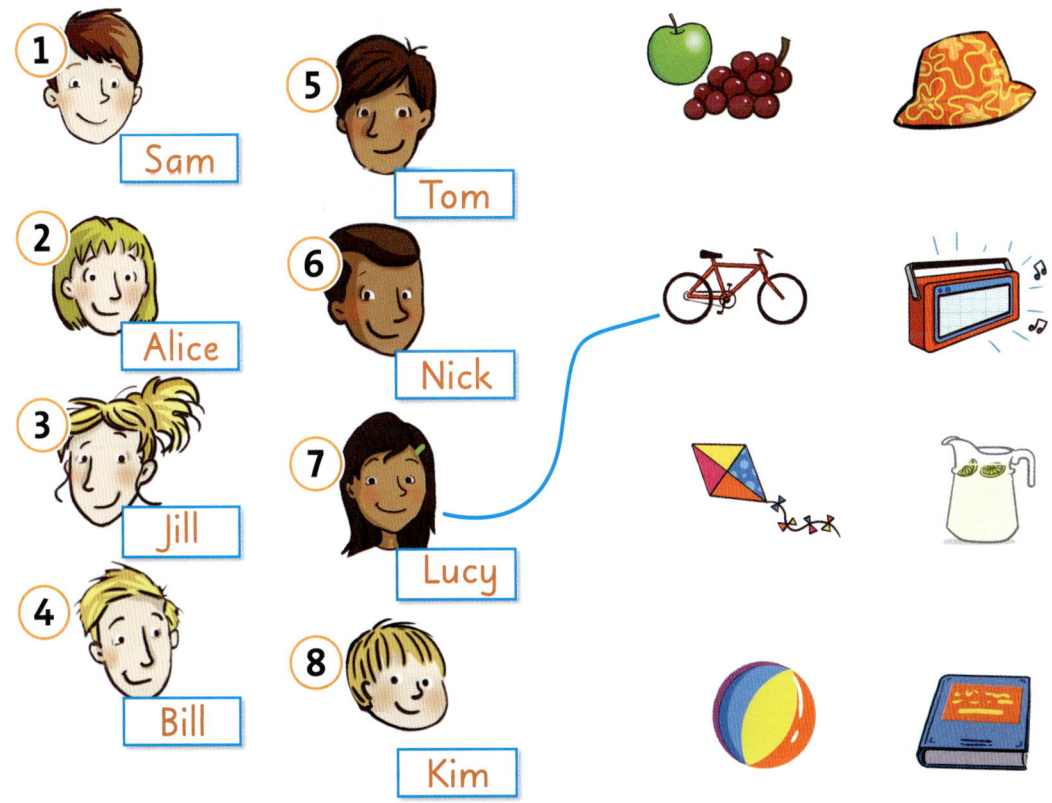

1 Sam
2 Alice
3 Jill
4 Bill
5 Tom
6 Nick
7 Lucy
8 Kim

3 Talk about the children.

The children are happy on the beach!

Yes, Lucy's got a bike to ride.

And Kim's got some fruit to eat.

UNIT 15 WORDS   see page 112

Story & writing

1 Listen and read. Then act. 🔊54

2 Write the words in the boxes and complete the words.

eating   ~~playing~~   jumping   finding

We're __playing__
t _e_ n _n_ _i_ _s_.

We're _____
in the s __ __.

We're _____
b __ r __ __ r s.

We're _____
s __ e __ __ s.

UNIT 15
WORDS   see page 112

Language practice

1 **Look and circle the letters to find the words.**

1	s	a	o	(l)	h
	b	(h)	(e)	c	(l)
2	r	e	p	p	r
	h	i	l	o	o
3	o	o	i	r	h
	b	e	a	t	d
4	l	e	n	r	o
	m	a	r	g	y
5	r	u	p	l	l
	p	a	e	e	r
6	s	e	a	r	l
	b	h	e	c	h
7	w	h	a	t	n
	t	r	e	i	r
8	l	l	r	r	n
	p	o	a	n	y
9	w	o	p	e	o
	h	a	t	p	r
10	r	a	r	e	o
	m	u	l	t	r
11	t	r	o	a	y
	b	o	e	t	s

2 **Do the speaking activity.** P 123

What colour's the shell?

It's blue.

Starters practice test

Look and read. Put a tick (✓) or a cross (✗) in the box.
There are two examples.

Examples

These are ships.

This is a flat.

Questions

1

This is the sea.

2

These are kites.

3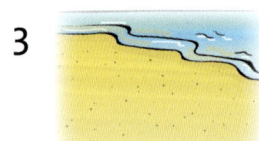

This is a beach.

4

These are jellyfish.

5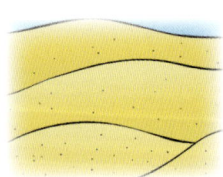

This is water.

Starters practice test

Listen and draw lines. There is one example. 🔊 55

Kim   Bill   Grace   Anna

Hugo   Eva   Nick

Revision 3

1 **Complete the adjectives crossword.**

① s

② c
a
r
y

This box is **small**.

REVISION 3 WORDS   see pages 108–112

2 Make sentences. Write numbers next to five of the pictures.

1 riding   He's   his   bike.

He's riding his bike.

2 They're   in   dresses   shop.   choosing   a

_____   [1]

3 the   cleaning   We're   car.

_____

4 in   the   She's   sea.   jumping

_____

5 children   school.   are   walking   The   to

_____

3 Colour the picture to find the animals.

gr = grey
w = white
br = brown
o = orange
g = green
bk = black
bl = blue
r = red
pn = pink
p = purple
w = white
y = yellow

4 Read, listen and circle. 🔊56

1  Which is my dad's motorbike?

(A)  (B)  (C)

2  What does Lucy want on her birthday cake?

(A)  (B)  (C)

3  What is Sam's favourite drink?

(A)  (B)  (C)

4  What's my teacher doing now?

(A)  (B)  (C)

1 **Look at the picture. Ask and answer these questions.**

Student A

1 Where's the kite?

2 What's the man on the beach doing?

3 What colour is the car?

Student B

1 Where are the shells?

2 How many children are there on the beach?

3 What colour is the ball?

2 **Look at the picture again. Ask and answer about these things.**

Student A

Student B

3 **Ask your teacher for the object cards. Take turns to ask and answer.**

Count the houses. How many are there?

There are three houses.

What colour ...?

What ...?

Where ...?

How many ...?

SPEAKING TEST **P** 107 and 108

Wordlist

Abbreviations

The following abbreviations have been used where it is necessary to show the part of speech:

n = noun   *v* = verb   *adj* = adjective   *pron* = pronoun   *prep* = preposition
s = singular   *p* = plural

Words marked with * are not on the Starters wordlist, but have been included for the sake of completeness.

Names

Boys: Alex Ben Bill Dan Hugo Mark Matt Nick Pat Sam Tom

Girls: Alice Anna Eva Grace Jill Kim Lucy May Pat Sue

Animals: Bouncer Chippy

Hello!

alphabet _____

and _____

apple _____

be _____

black _____

blue _____

boat _____

box _____

brown _____

cat _____

dog _____

eighteen _____

elephant _____

fifteen _____

fish (*s*) _____

flower _____

fourteen _____

giraffe _____

green _____

grey _____

hat _____

hello _____

house _____

How many? _____

How old? _____

ice cream _____

juice _____

kite _____

letter (*alphabet*) _____

listen _____

lorry _____

mouse (*animal*) _____

name _____

night _____

nineteen _____

one _____

orange (*adj*) _____

orange (*n*) _____

pink _____

plane _____

purple _____

question mark* _____

red _____

robot _____

say _____

seventeen _____

sixteen _____

sun _____

three _____

tree _____

twenty _____

two _____

umbrella* _____

vegetables* _____

watermelon _____

white _____

with _____

yellow _____

zoo _____

1 I love animals!

animal _____

bee _____

bird _____

chicken _____

colour (n) _____

colour (v) _____

cow _____

do _____

donkey _____

duck _____

fish (s + pl) _____

frog _____

goat _____

horse _____

in _____

know _____

look _____

mice _____

next to _____

not _____

on _____

sheep (s+pl) _____

this _____

where _____

Wow! _____

2 At home

armchair _____

ask _____

at _____

bath _____

bathroom _____

bed _____

bedroom _____

behind _____

between _____

bookcase _____

clock _____

computer _____

cupboard _____

dining room _____

door _____

floor _____

garden _____

hall _____

home _____

in front of _____

kitchen _____

lamp _____

living room _____

mat _____

mirror _____

Mum _____

pardon _____

phone (n) _____

picture _____

radio _____

right _____

rug _____

room _____

sofa _____

table _____

television _____

under _____

wall _____

which _____

window _____

3 Family and friends

baby _____

big _____

boy _____

brother _____

dad _____

family _____

father _____

friend _____

funny _____

girl _____

grandfather _____

grandmother _____

happy _____

have got _____

his _____

mother _____

old _____

sad _____

scary _____

pet _____

silly _____

sister _____

small _____

year _____

young _____

4 Food!

banana _____

beans _____

bread _____

breakfast _____

burger _____

carrot _____

chips _____

coconut _____

dinner _____

eat _____

egg _____

evening _____

favourite _____

food _____

fruit _____

grapes _____

kiwi _____

lemon _____

like (v) _____

lime _____

lunch _____

mango _____

meal* _____

meat _____

meatballs _____

onion _____

pear _____

peas _____

pie _____

pineapple _____

please _____

potato _____

rice _____

thanks _____

that _____

tomato _____

would like _____

5 I like clothes

bag _____

baseball cap _____

boots _____

clothes _____

dress _____

glasses _____

handbag _____

hat _____

hold _____

jacket _____

jeans _____

shirt _____

shoes _____

shorts _____

skirt _____

socks _____

thing* _____

today _____

trousers _____

T-shirt _____

watch (n) _____

wear _____

6 Look at us!

alien _____

arm _____

beautiful _____

body _____

doll _____

ear _____

eye _____

face _____

foot/feet _____

Great! _____

hair _____

hand _____

head _____

leg _____

let's (v) _____

monkey _____

monster _____

mouth _____

nose _____

person _____

play (v) _____

see _____

short _____

smile (v) _____

snake _____

spider _____

tail _____

teddy bear _____

then _____

tiger _____

toy _____

ugly _____

(7) We love school!

board _____

book _____

boy _____

children _____

classmates _____

classroom _____

colour (v) _____

come _____

crayon _____

down* _____

draw _____

English _____

girl _____

good _____

kids _____

keyboard
  (computer) _____

learn _____

lots of/
  a lot of _____

make _____

man _____

mouse
  (computer) _____

now _____

painting _____

page _____

paper _____

pen _____

pencil _____

pick up _____

point (v) _____

poster _____

rubber _____

ruler _____

school _____

show _____

sit (v) _____

sleep _____

some _____

stand (v) _____

talk _____

teacher _____

up* _____

word _____

work* (n) _____

write _____

(8) In the playground

answer (v) _____

badminton _____

ball (n) _____

baseball _____

basketball _____

bike (n) _____

bounce (v) _____

can (v) _____

catch (v) _____

football _____

here _____

hit (v) _____

hockey _____

kick (v) _____

playground _____

ride (v) _____

run (v) _____

sport _____

table tennis _____

tennis _____

throw (v) _____

too _____

walk (v) _____

(9) My hobbies

board game _____

cake _____

double (adj) _____

enjoy (v) _____

fish (v) _____

guitar _____

hobby (n) _____

jump (v) _____

love (v) _____

music _____

paint (v) _____

park (n) _____

piano _____

read _____

sea _____

sing _____

song _____

spell (v) _____

story _____

swim (*v*) _____

10 Your day

about _____

afternoon _____

again _____

bed _____

day _____

English (*n*) _____

get _____

go to bed _____

go to sleep _____

goodbye _____

have _____

lesson _____

morning _____

paint (*v*) _____

painting (*n*) _____

11 In the street

angry _____

bus _____

car _____

child _____

class _____

clean (*adj*) _____

clean (*v*) _____

closed _____

dirty _____

fly (*v*) _____

go (*v*) _____

helicopter _____

her _____

motorbike _____

Mr _____

Mrs _____

new _____

nice _____

open (*adj*) _____

people _____

sad _____

ship _____

shop _____

street _____

train _____

wave (*v*) _____

women _____

12 My grandparents

cousin _____

Don't worry! _____

flat _____

grandma _____

grandpa _____

grandparents* _____

mother _____

13 Going to the zoo

bear _____

choose _____

crocodile _____

drink (*v*) _____

great (*adj*) _____

hippo _____

lizard _____

photo _____

polar bear _____

take _____

these _____

those _____

tiger _____

zebra _____

zoo _____

14 Happy birthday!

balloon _____

bat _____

camera _____

chocolates _____

lemonade _____

milk _____

mine _____

party* _____

present _____

See you! _____

skateboard _____

tablet _____

tennis racket _____

whose _____

15 At the beach

beach _____

find _____

jellyfish _____

sand _____

shell _____